AMERICA
Online

Wired in a Week

AMERICA
Online

Wired
in a
Week

Get Online &
Do More Online in
**Just 10 Minutes
a Day!**

Regina Lewis

AOL Online Advisor

An AOL Time Warner Company

Warner Books, Inc., 1271 Avenue of the Americas, New York, NY 10020

Visit our Web site at www.twbookmark.com. For information on Time Warner Trade Publishing's online publishing program, visit www.ipublish.com.

 An AOL Time Warner Company

Printed in the United States of America

First Printing: January 2002

10 9 8 7 6 5 4 3

ISBN: 0-446-67913-5
LCCN: 2001095989

AOL Online Advisor & *Wired in a Week* author Regina Lewis at work.

Acknowledgments

● ●

This book is inspired by, and written for, the millions of people looking to get online and do more online and anyone who is still on the fence...

Special thanks to Jeff Corbett for helping to put it all on paper.

Contents

● ●

Introduction

*Your Internet experience is
what you make of it.*

Almost by definition, we're all new at the "Internet thing." Including me. Make no mistake, I am not a "techie" and appreciate the fact that most of us grew up with TVs and telephones... not computers.

The challenge becomes: How do I get online? And, once I do, where do I go from there? My goal is to help address both those questions without getting too technical.

So, whether you've just signed on to the AOL service for the first time or you're a longtime member looking to get the most out of AOL 7.0 (maybe you're somewhere in between), we hope this book is a helpful guide.

I strongly believe your Internet experience is what you make of it and that the online phenomenon is about people and the impact the medium is having on their everyday life. There's never been a more important time to be "connected."

When you find out you can communicate instantly with friends and family around the world and score some of the best shopping bargains online, you want to know more. When you learn that your local school district can be wired to the Internet for free, you can't wait to jot down the facts. When you discover some grandparents receive photos of their grandchildren online every week, you want to be that grandparent.

It's a matter of telling the stories and explaining the features in a way that is approachable and easy-to-follow. *Wired in a Week* aims to do just that. If you have a computer, a phone jack and/or high-speed access and this book, you're good to go.

Let's get going...

Get Started

Registration Process

If you're already an AOL member, skip ahead to Day 1 and find out more about getting help online. Also, check out high-speed access options on page 65.

You can use the enclosed CD to upgrade to AOL version 7.0 if you haven't already — it's free and takes a matter of minutes.

For everyone else, let's start at the beginning. If you follow the steps outlined on the next few pages, you'll be up and running online in about ten minutes.

Step One: Get your computer "wired"

After your computer is unpacked and assembled, you need to connect your modem to a phone line. Your modem is the part of your computer that enables you to access the Internet.

The modem on most computers connects to the Internet through the same type of jack and telephone cord that connects your phone to the wall. Consult your computer manual to find the modem connection on your computer and plug the phone cord into it.

Plug the other end of the cord into an available phone jack in the wall. You may need to unplug a phone line to free up a jack and reconnect your phone when you're not online. If you have two phone lines, use the second line for your computer.

If you have high-speed Internet connections (like cable or DSL), your cable provider or phone company has already hooked up your connection to the Internet.

AOL High-Speed Broadband service offers Internet access through various regional partners. You can find out more about high-speed options (sometimes referred to as "broadband") when you get up and running online and by scanning options outlined on page 65.

Step Two: Learn to use the "mouse"

All computers come with a mouse. It's an oval device connected by a cord to your desktop computer, or a ball or touch pad on a laptop.

The mouse allows you to control the computer by clicking one of the buttons on the mouse — usually the left button. You should consult your computer manual to learn how to plug in and use your mouse. If your computer is on and your hand is on the mouse, you can roll the mouse around on a flat surface.

You might also want to use a mouse pad — a little place mat designed to provide extra traction and control. As you roll the mouse around, you'll see a small symbol, usually an arrow, move around your screen.

As you move the cursor around the screen and over selected pictures or text called "hyperlinks," the cursor will change into a hand with a pointed index finger — simply "click" on these areas to begin exploring all of the great features available on the AOL service. While you are connecting to different areas of the AOL service or sites on the Internet, the cursor will momentarily turn into an hourglass.

Step Three: Install the software

Now it's time to put the AOL 7.0 CD into the appropriate drive on your computer so you can sign up for membership. Turn on your computer and insert the AOL CD into the CD-ROM drive on your computer. Your computer will automatically "open" the AOL installation program and will go through a series of steps.

First, the AOL installation screen will appear on your screen asking you to click on one of the boxes (also referred to as a "button") if you are a new member and another if you are a current member.

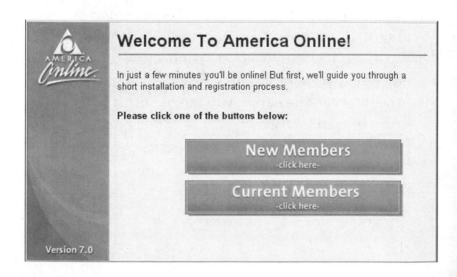

Click on the appropriate one, and we're on our way. As the installation process proceeds, you will periodically be asked to click on the **Next** button to approve what the software is doing and move on to the next step. Clicking **Next** at each step will result in a safe, successful installation. When in doubt, click **Next**.

Step Four: Select an access number

After proceeding through a few screens, you will come to a new screen where you will be asked to select the phone number the AOL service will use to connect you to the Internet.

You will first be asked to enter your area code, so the system can locate access numbers in your area. Type it in and click **Next**.

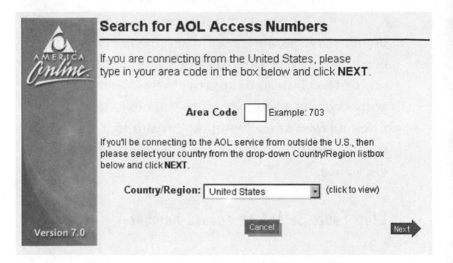

Search for AOL Access Numbers

If you are connecting from the United States, please type in your area code in the box below and click **NEXT**.

Area Code ☐ Example: 703

If you'll be connecting to the AOL service from outside the U.S., then please select your country from the drop-down Country/Region listbox below and click **NEXT**.

Country/Region: United States ▾ (click to view)

Cancel   Next▶

Version 7.0

If you have call waiting, you will be prompted to select a special calling option so incoming calls will not interrupt your online connection.

You'll also be asked to indicate if you need to dial "9" to reach an outside line. From there, click **Next** again and your computer will connect to AOL for the first time.

You'll hear a sustained honking sound that lasts a few seconds. This sound tells you the modem is working. You should hear it every time you connect to the AOL service unless you are using a high-speed connection.

Soon you'll see a list of available access numbers in your area. Review the list and choose the number that is closest to you. Once you have chosen a number, click on it once to select it. You will see a red check mark appear. If available, it's a good idea to choose at least two local phone numbers.

If you're not certain which numbers are local calls for you, check with your phone company to be sure. Then click **Next** again, and move on to Step Five. **Tip:** When traveling, you can change the AOL access number to a local number so that you don't incur long distance charges.

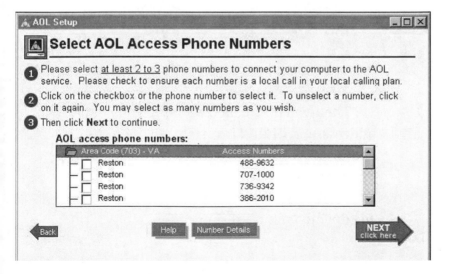

Step Five: Register your account

After you've finished setting up your access numbers, it's time to register for your AOL account. You'll be asked to type in the registration number and password found on the AOL CD packaging.

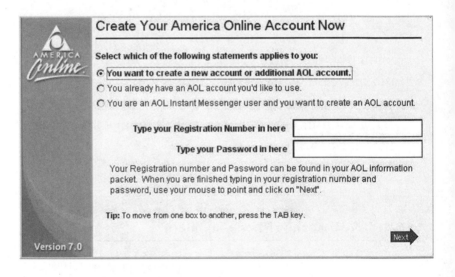

Then you'll be asked to enter your name, address, and billing information, including the credit card or checking account number you want to use for your new subscription. Remember, you won't be charged a monthly fee during your trial time.

This information is strictly confidential
and we use the most advanced cutting-edge
technology available to protect your privacy.
AOL has the highest standards for privacy
and security and will never give out your
credit card number or any other personal,
demographic, or financial information without your express permission.

You will also be asked to accept AOL's
Terms of Service agreement, designed to help
ensure a safe and secure experience for all
AOL members. We ask all new members to
agree to AOL's Community Guidelines. It's all
part of taking pride in, and protecting, the
AOL community and includes treating other
AOL members with respect and avoiding vul-
gar or hurtful language. Thanks in advance
for doing your part.

Step Six: Pick a screen name and password

This final step sets the stage for your
cyberspace debut. It's time to pick your AOL
screen name and password. Your screen

name will be your e-mail address (the one you give out to family and friends) so consider choosing a name that is easy for you to remember and for friends to recognize.

It can combine letters, numbers and blank spaces. Screen names are a bit like vanity license plates, so be creative. If you want to be businesslike, it can be an initial and your last name.

America Online has more than 31 million members. Many utilize multiple screen names — you get seven with each membership — so don't be surprised if your first choice is taken. You may be given alternative suggestions or asked to try another combination if you don't get the screen name you'd like right away.

Keep experimenting and you're likely to find one that's available and works for you, especially since AOL screen names can be up to 16 alphanumeric characters long.

Because there's such a run on screen names, I even reserve them for my children as soon as they're born. I'm hoping they'll think that's cool of me when they grow up.

When you click on the **Create a Screen Name** button, the AOL service will ask if this screen name is for a child. If the new screen name is for a child, click on **Yes** to proceed to some important information for parents.

You can then walk through the steps to set the appropriate parental control level for your child to have a safe and enjoyable online experience. If the screen name is not for a child, click on the **No** button to continue.

Once you are up and running, parental controls can grow with your child. Visit AOL Keyword: **Parental Controls** for more information.

After you've chosen your screen name, it's time to choose a **password**. This should be a combination of letters and numbers. Consider it as confidential as your ATM bank card PIN or other secret codes.

Sign up by phone

If you run into any difficulty registering for AOL on your own, or if you feel more comfortable speaking with someone directly and talking through the process, please feel free to call 1-800-4-ONLINE and ask to **Sign Up By Phone**. A customer service representative will help you establish an AOL Screen Name and password in a matter of minutes. You will also be informed about your AOL introductory offer and will receive a New Member Software Kit in a few days via U.S. Mail. For more information about getting customer service help 24 hours a day, 7 days a week, online and by phone, see the "Getting Help" resources outlined in Day 1.

CONGRATULATIONS! Get ready for tomorrow by calling a few close friends or family members and asking for their e-mail addresses.

That's it. You've done it!

DAY 1

Get in Touch & Get Help

Your online experience will begin with what may be the four most famous words in cyberspace: "Welcome! You've Got Mail!"

The first page you will see is the AOL "Welcome Screen" — one of the most popular pages in cyberspace — providing access to popular AOL content and features.

The Welcome Screen and other content areas on the AOL service are automatically updated throughout the day, offering the most timely information available. For that reason, some of the illustrations in this book may not look exactly as they do on your computer screen.

If you have time, explore a little bit. Use the mouse to click on text and graphics on the screen. There are no "mistakes" when you're exploring online and you can't hurt anything, so don't feel intimidated. When you're done looking around, let's send your first e-mail.

 ## E-mail - electronic mail

E-mail (electronic mail) has totally revolutionized the way people communicate with one another, making it easier than ever to stay in touch. Consider the great advantages of e-mail:

☞ It's free.
☞ Messages can be short or long.
☞ You can send e-mail to more than one person at a time.

☞ You can send e-mail around the world in just seconds.

☞ You can read e-mail whenever it's most convenient.

☞ You can attach/insert pictures and documents.

 Let's do it - sending e-mail

Do you have e-mail addresses for family and friends? Write them on a Post-it note and attach it to your computer for now. Let's start by sending e-mail.

Now click your mouse on the **Write** 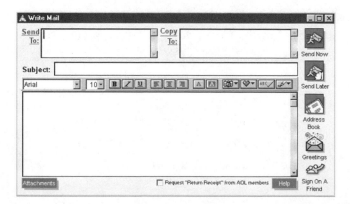 paper-and-pencil icon on the AOL Toolbar — located at the top of the screen, the second icon from the left. An e-mail screen like the one below will appear.

If you don't have someone's e-mail address or if you just want to try it out, send an e-mail to yourself. Since you're on the AOL service, there's no need to include the "@aol.com" part of your address.

If you're writing to someone who's not an AOL member, you need to type in their entire Internet address, including the "@" sign and the part following it, which usually ends in .com or .net (e.g., jsmith@mars.com).

When the blank e-mail form appears, your cursor will be in the "Send To" box. Now, type in one of the addresses from your list.

Want to send mail to more than one AOL member and non-AOL member at a time? In that case, just put a comma after the first e-mail address, add the second, and continue like this:

When you're done addressing your letter,
move on to the "Subject" box either by pressing the **Tab** key twice on your keyboard or by
clicking your mouse anywhere in the "Subject" box.

What you type here will appear in the
recipients' e-mail inboxes, along with your e-
mail address, so that they can tell who the
message is from and what it's about. For now,
just type "Hello."

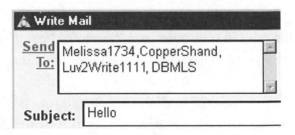

Now we're ready to move on to the main
body of the message. Move your cursor to
the large box at the bottom of the e-mail
form, either by clicking your mouse there or
pressing **Tab** on the keyboard.

Then begin to type away. A good message
for now might be "This is my new e-mail
address. I'm wired!!!!! Please write back. Bye

for now." Your e-mail should now look like this:

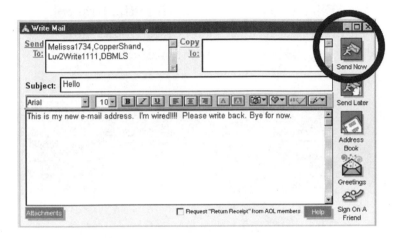

When you're finished writing you might want to spell check your message by clicking on the spell check [ABC✓] icon. Next, click the **Send Now** button in the top right corner of the e-mail form. A box will pop up saying it has been sent. Click on the **OK** button.

If you're like most AOL members, this will be the first of many e-mails you'll send.

How do you know if someone read the e-mail?

Click on the word **Mail** from the first column on the toolbar. Select **Read Mail** then click on **Sent Mail** from the pull-down menu.

Then highlight the item of mail in the **Sent Mail** listing and click on the **Status** box at the bottom of the screen.

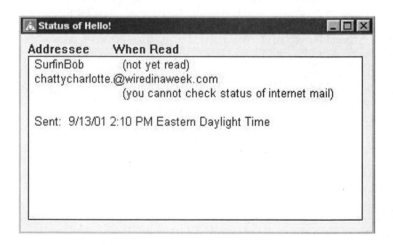

If the e-mail was sent and opened by an AOL member, you will see the date and time it was read. If it's not yet been read, it will simply say, "not read yet." This feature does not work for e-mail sent to non-AOL members.

Receiving and responding to e-mail

Most AOL members sign on several times a week and spend an average of over an hour a day online, so it probably won't take long before one or more of your recipients write back.

You'll know you've got an e-mail when you hear those three magic words you'll soon come to love — "You've Got Mail" — coming from your computer speakers.

At the same time, the mailbox icon at the far left of the AOL Toolbar will change to show the red-letter flag icon standing up.

Empty Mailbox

"You've Got Mail!"

To read your mail, click on the **mailbox** icon, and your e-mail inbox will appear. If you have more than one message waiting, it will look like this:

Double-click on the message you want to read and the e-mail form will come up. After you read the message, you can easily send your reply.

Click on the **Reply** button at the top right corner of the e-mail and a new e-mail form will appear with the "Send To" and "Subject" boxes already filled out. If you received a note that was sent to more than one person and you want to reply to the entire group, click on **Reply All** instead of **Reply.**

Type in your message and send it, just like a new e-mail and it will instantly appear in others' e-mail boxes.

Downloading attachments

You've Got Mail — but guess what, a file is attached. Don't panic — it is easy to download and open. If your best friend sends an e-mail with that famous cheesecake recipe attached, your mailbox will look like this:

Open the e-mail message. Click on the **Download** button located in the lower left corner of the screen. You will see two options: **Download Now** or **Download Later**.

The next screen you will see is a warning box asking if you know the person who sent the attached file and if you still want to download it.

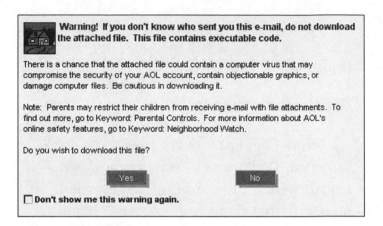

If you are sure the file is safe to download, click **Yes.** The next box that appears will ask you if you want to save this file to the Download Manager. Click **Save,** but before you do, write down or memorize the name of the file you are downloading.

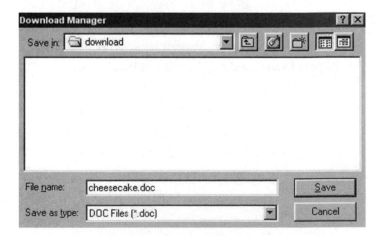

After you've downloaded a file, the AOL service will ask if you want to locate that file. Click **Yes** and browse through the file library to retrieve it.

File name

E-mail tips and tricks

With AOL 7.0, there are all kinds of new ways to give the next e-mail you send some personality. Click on **Mail Center** on the AOL Toolbar for these and other options:

Color. Mix and match more than 48 color choices for e-mail typefaces and backgrounds. You can even customize your own colors. Blue type, yellow background . . . the combinations are limitless.

Writing style. YOUR HANDWRITING ISN'T LIKE everyone else's and your e-mail writing style doesn't have to be either. With AOL 7.0, you can now choose from more than 100 font *choices and 16-point sizes everything from casual to formal and from* **BIG** to SMALL.

Accent. Put some punch in your point by **bolding**, *italicizing*, and <u>underlining</u> words. ***<u>Or use all three at once</u>***.

Mail art. Want to send flowers, a birthday cake, seashells or a kiss? Bring your e-mail to a whole new level with these easy-to-add images and sounds. Click on the **Mail** icon on the toolbar and select **Mail Extras** from the drop-down menu. You'll be surprised how many choices there are.

Hyperlinks. If there's something online you'd love to share, send a direct "link." Just click and drag the heart icon from the upper right corner of the screen into the message you are writing. And *Voila*, a blue hyperlink (e.g., <u>Mail Extras</u>) will instantly appear in your e-mail, allowing the recipient simply to click on the link and go directly to that site or feature.

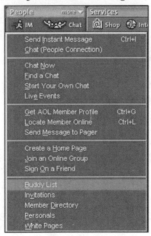 Your buddy list

Now that you've got the hang of e-mail, it's time to move on to instant messaging. The first step is to setup a directory of your online friends and family with the "Buddy List" feature which will let you know when your online friends — your "buddies" — are online at the same time you are.

If your Buddy List is not up on your

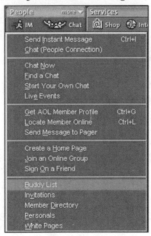

screen now, you can bring it up by clicking on the **People** icon on the toolbar. Select **Buddy List**. Your Buddy List will pop up on the screen. Before it is set up, it looks like this:

 Let's do it - setting up your buddy list

To start entering your buddies, click on the **Setup** button at the bottom of the Buddy List window. Another window will pop up showing three "folders" in which you can place your buddies. For now, use only the "Buddies" folder. Click on the **Add Buddy** button at the bottom of the screen to enter a name.

Enter your buddy's AOL screen name, click the **Save** button, and he/she will be added to the list. Repeat the process with the next name. When you are done entering buddies, click on the **Return To Buddy List** button at the bottom left of the window.

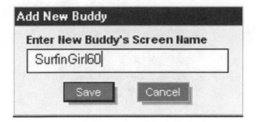

You will most likely notice that some of the screen names you entered don't appear on the list. That is because not all of those people are online right now. Only those buddies who are currently online will show up on your list, so you know they're available to receive instant messages.

If a screen name on your Buddy List is in parenthesis — like this: (ReginaLewis) — your buddy just signed off. If it has an asterisk next to it — like this: ReginaLewis* — he or she just signed on.

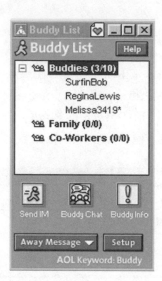

The numbers in parenthesis at the top of the list tells you how many buddies you have, and how many are currently online. If it says (3/10), that means that you have a total of 10 buddies and that three of them are currently online.

When you want to let people know you've stepped away from your computer, click on the Away Message button on your Buddy List and then select an away message option or customize one of your own.

The notepad symbol displayed in your buddy list means the person is indicating that they've stepped away from their computer. The notepad will let people know why you're not responding to instant messages.

Now that your buddy list has been created, let's take a look at instant messaging.

Instant messaging - lives up to its name!
IM

Instant messages are just what they sound like. You write a message, press **Send**, and your note pops up on the other person's computer screen — right away — in a little box that looks like this:

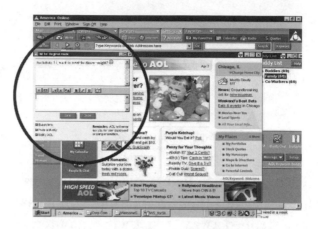

Instant messages let you carry on a conversation online just as quickly and easily as you could with a person sitting across the table.

You can "IM" — it's pronounced "eye-em" and is the nickname for instant messaging — with a friend while you check sports scores, look for movie listings or do anything else online.

It's best to keep IMs short. Long messages are better suited for e-mail. If you're already a big IMer, we've got some "secrets" for you too.

If you have friends who use other online services, they can IM with you — at no cost to either of you. Go to AOL Keyword: **AIM** to

send them information on how they can sign
up free for AOL Instant Messenger.

 ## Let's do it - sending &
receiving IMs

Now that you have your Buddy List set
up, you're ready to enter the world of instant
messaging. If you end up doing one thing
online more than any other, this might just
be it.

Choose one of your buddies who is online,
or call a friend and tell them to sign on. Click
once on their screen name and then click the
Send IM button at the bottom of the Buddy
List (you can save time by simply double-
clicking on their screen name). An instant
message form like this will appear.

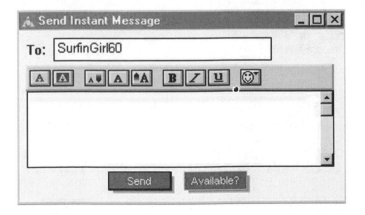

Your cursor will already be in the larger box in the lower half of the form. Type a quick message and click on the **Send** button.

It's that simple. Your buddy's computer will make a quick bell sound to let them know he/she has a message and your IM will appear on their screen.

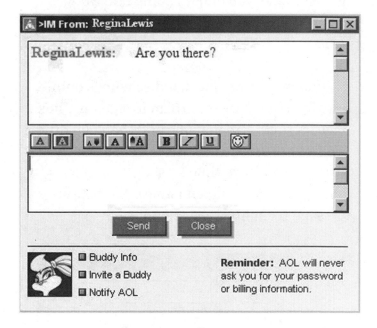

Responding to an instant message is just as simple as sending one. Click on the button and the window will add a second box. That's where you can type your response.

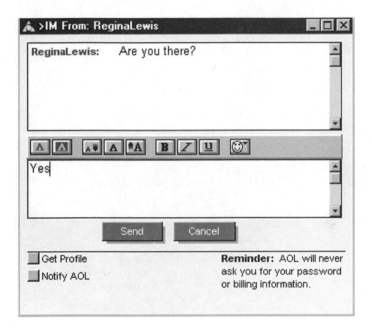

Type your message in the bottom box, then click **Send** and it will appear like this on both your screen and your buddy's.

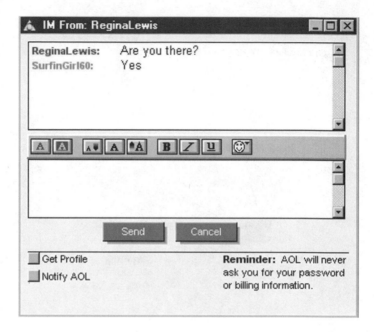

Now you can keep going back and forth as long as you like. As you are typing on the bottom half of the window, the text appears only on your screen.

When you click on the **Send** button, it will be added to the top half of the window on both screens. You can read back through the text of the entire conversation using the up and down arrows at the right side of the window.

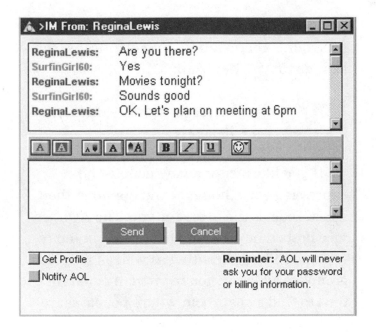

Instant messaging is so popular it's spawned a language all its own. Here are some fun, short phrases and symbols you can use again and again:

- AYT-Are you there?
- G2G-Got to go
- CYA-See Ya
- AFK-Away from keyboard
- BRB-Be right back
- BAK-Back at keyboard
- LOL-Laughing out loud
- ROFL-Rolling on the floor, laughing
- IMHO-In my humble opinion
- IMNSHO-In my not so humble opinion
- BTW-By the way
- GMTA-Great minds think alike
- :)-smile
- ;)-wink
- :(-frown
- {}-hug
- :*-kiss

For more information on AOL instant messaging, abbreviations and emoticons (smilies), go to AOL Keyword: **LOL**.

Chat/message boards - express your thoughts

If you like meeting new people and expressing your thoughts and opinions, then a chat room is the place for you. The AOL service hosts thousands of chat rooms on topics from politics to parenting as well as support groups of all kinds. You're virtually guaranteed to find a chat room where people share your interests.

Chatting moves quickly, so if you'd prefer to take your time expressing your opinion or reading what others have to say, check out the message boards.

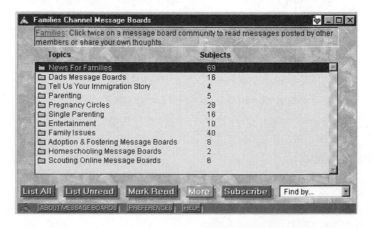

Message boards are similar to chat rooms, but the conversation doesn't take place in "real time." Throughout the AOL service you'll come across opportunities to review and contribute to message boards, which is like "posting" a message on a bulletin board.

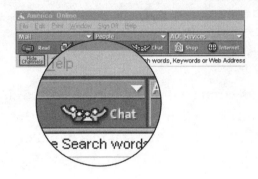

Chatting is one of the most popular activities on AOL — to the tune of 10 million hours per week! The first step is to find a chat interest by going to the People Connection, AOL's home for chat. To get there, click on the **Chat** icon located on the toolbar. This will take you to the People Connection channel, which looks like this:

To search through the list of active chats, click on **Find a Chat** at the left side of the screen. This will bring you to a menu of the available chats.

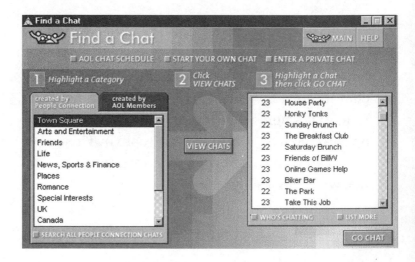

Look through the list of categories on the left-hand side of the window and highlight one that interests you by clicking on it once.

Then click on the **View Chats** button in the middle of the screen and a list of chats in that area will appear on the right-hand side of the screen.

The chat room window has three main parts. The largest box is the area where the chat is actually going on. It's usually a good idea to follow the conversation for a little while before jumping right in so you can see what people are talking about.

The box along the right-hand side of the window shows a list of people who are currently in the chat room.

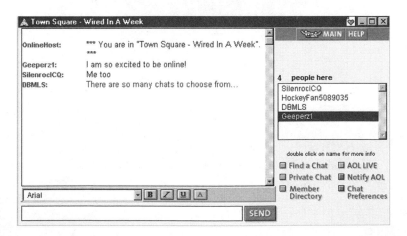

When ready to participate in the chat, click on the box at the bottom of the screen to put your cursor there and then type what you'd like to say.

When you're finished typing, click on the **Send** button and your message will appear as part of the chat. Everyone who has entered this room will be able to see what you have written after you click the **Send** button.

To leave a chat room, click on the ☒ at the top right corner of the window to close it. The "Find a Chat" menu will be visible.

Note: Because chat rooms are public forums, as in any public place there are all kinds of people and you never know who you're going to run into.

The good news is, when you're online, you have the control. If you are in a chat room and someone is bothering you, you can double-click on their name and select **Ignore Member.**

☐ **Ignore Member**

You will no longer see messages from that member.

New member areas

If you're new to the AOL service, a great place to visit is the AOL Member Welcome Center. Here, you'll find easy-to-follow slide shows that cover all of the basics — from the AOL Welcome Screen to AOL's content channels, e-mail, instant messaging, online shopping and more! Visit AOL Keyword: **Welcome Center.**

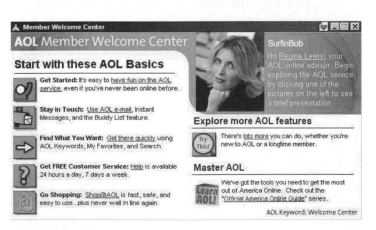

Another great area for "newbies" and AOL veterans alike can be found at AOL Keyword: **Save Time**. Here you will find the best of the AOL service conveniently packaged into categories designed to help simplify your life.

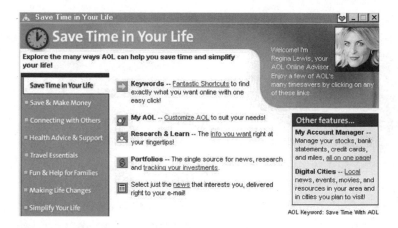

Get AOL Tips delivered directly to your e-mail box by subscribing to the popular AOL Insider Tips Newsletter. This free newsletter is packed with AOL secrets, shortcuts, and insider tips for getting the most out of your favorite AOL features. Visit AOL Keyword: **Insider Tips** to subscribe.

Getting help online

It's bound to happen. Sometimes you just need help, especially when trying things for the first time. The AOL service prides itself on being easy to use and that means making sure help is always free and accessible — online and offline.

Fortunately, on the AOL service, help is literally only a click away. Where to click? Simple — anywhere it says **Help** — at the right-hand side of the Toolbar, on the bottom of your e-mail screen at AOL Keyword: **Help**

(more on Keywords on Day 2) and wherever
else indicated. From there, you'll see various
help topics of interest with links to step-by-
step instructions.

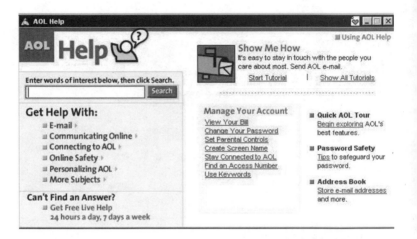

Online help resources are great for begin-
ners and advanced computer users alike, not
only for solving problems, but also for learning more about the AOL service.

You'll be amazed how many different
things you can find out how to do just by
clicking on different help topics. Popular topics and frequently asked questions (FAQs)
include: downloading files and e-mail attachments and "How Can I Recover E-Mail I
Recently Deleted?"

One of the best things about getting online help is — if you only have one phone line — you don't have to sign off to call for help on the telephone. You can even get free, one-on-one customer support via e-mail.

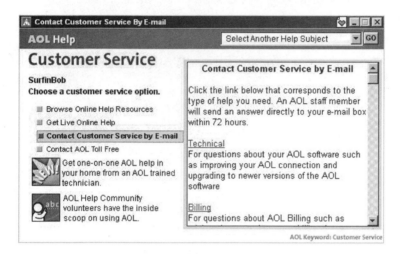

Of course, if you'd prefer to talk with someone, you can always call our customer service centers toll free, 24 hours a day, seven days a week at 1-800-901-9795.

You can even update and view your AOL account billing information online — it's fast, easy and secure. Go to AOL Keyword: **Billing.** To find other telephone access numbers in your area at AOL Keyword: **Access.**

AOL in home support

For your added convenience, the AOL service is now offering AOL In Home Support. Upon request, an AOL trained technician will come to your house to setup, register, and/or demonstrate use of the AOL service on AOL products or devices. AOL In Home Support prices vary for different services.

To find out more about AOL In Home Support and the availability of service in your area, please visit AOL Keywords: **IHS** or **In Home Support**. This area will provide you with the latest details about AOL In Home Support. There is also a form to request the service.

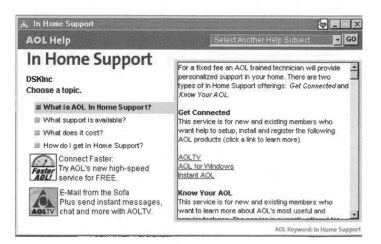

Sign off

Click your cursor on the words **Sign Off** on
the toolbar — the ruler-like box with text and
graphics at the top of the screen. A pull-down
menu will appear. Move your cursor down to
the words **Sign Off** on the pull-down menu
and click again.

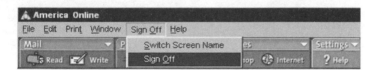

You'll hear the word "Good-bye" and know
your session is over. The Sign Off/Sign On
screen will appear. Wow, we've covered a lot
in one day. On Day 2 we will sign on again and
begin searching and surfing.

SECRETS DAY 1

· **Sign on:** You can sign on to the AOL service from any computer that has AOL installed on it. Just click on the drop-down arrow on the right-hand side and scroll down to **Guest**. Sign-on and when asked, enter your screen name and password. (You can also access your e-mail on the Internet at www.aol.com.)

· **Sign on a friend:** Here's the deal. If you sign up a friend for the AOL service, you'll not only get another name to add to your Buddy List, you'll get cash as well. Not bad. Just go to AOL Keyword: **Friend** and enter your friend or relative's name and address. We'll send them a free AOL CD. If they use the CD to join AOL and stick with the service, you'll be rewarded.

· **Write down your password:** Soon you'll know it like the back of your hand, but for now it's best to write it down and keep it tucked away somewhere safe.

· **Stay in touch with e-mail and instant messages:** Sure, you often want to hear your friend or family member's voice, but if you talk to someone regularly on the phone, try chatting online half or even one quarter of the time. You could save big money on phone bills.

· **Instant message icons:** On AOL 7.0, if you click on the **Setup** button on your Buddy List, next click on **Preferences**, then click on the **Instant Messages** tab, you will find many fun Instant Message options. You can select buddy icons to display to other AOL members, timestamp your IMs even send smiley faces as art. As with most AOL secrets, the fun begins with exploring the possibilities.

· **Add a personal touch with e-mail signatures:** Signatures are a great shortcut for adding a personal touch to e-mails. Click on the **pencil** icon above and to the right of your e-mail text. Then click **Set Up Signatures** and **Create** on the ensuing screen. Now you can create as many e-mail signatures as you want. To add one to your e-mail, click on the **pencil** icon again.

· **Storing your e-mail:** Use your **Personal Filing Cabinet** to store e-mail you have sent and received and to keep a record of downloaded files and newsgroup postings. From the **Set-**

tings menu on the AOL toolbar, select **Preferences**, then click on **Filing Cabinet**. You can
quickly search the contents of your Filing
Cabinet by clicking on **Find**. You'll be able to
sift through both the subject lines and the
content of your e-mail to easily locate what
you're looking for. For more information on
how to use your Personal Filing Cabinet, visit
AOL Keyword: **PFC**.

· **Retrieving (unsending) e-mail:** You can
retrieve (unsend) an e-mail message if the e-
mail was sent only to America Online screen
names; and none of the recipients of the e-
mail has opened the e-mail. Bring up your
Mailbox, click on the **Sent Mail** tab, then click
on the e-mail that you want to unsend. Now
click on the **Unsend** button on the bottom of
your mailbox.

· **Undeleting e-mail:** If you accidentally
delete an e-mail that you wanted to keep,
click on the **Mail Center** icon on your AOL
Toolbar and select **Recently Deleted Mail**.
From this list you can retrieve deleted e-mails
from the last 24 hours only.

· **Blind copy:** There may be times when you want to send the same e-mail to many people, but you don't necessarily want everyone to know which e-mail addresses received the e-mail. By using parenthesis around an e-mail address inside of the Copy To: box, you can hide that address from everyone else. You can practice by blind copying yourself first like this: (ReginaLewis).

· **Privacy:** If you click on the **Setup** button at the bottom of your Buddy List, next click on **Preferences,** then click on the **Privacy** tab (or **Privacy Preferences** button), you will find a series of privacy options. You can choose to block people from IM'ing you or just prevent your Screen Name from appearing on their Buddy List. Review the options closely to see if there are any that might improve your online experience.

· **Learn from a buddy:** While we've asked for 10 minutes a day, getting a friend who's already on the AOL service to show you around can save time and make your online experience even more rewarding right from the start.

Netiquette 101

Mama always said — wait, we didn't have a computer growing up and Mom never covered this. When the subject is online etiquette, we're in unchartered territory.

For the most part, cyberspace is a pretty easygoing place. The general rule of thumb is "No harm, no foul." But knowing the DOs and DON'Ts of cyberspace is like having good table manners. There may be times when you can forget them, but it's generally wise to keep them in mind. So consider this Online Etiquette 101:

If you don't have something nice to say...

Don't say it, and for goodness sake, don't put it in writing. Candid conversation makes sense online, but use good judgment. An offhand remark behind someone's back is just one click away from being forwarded and landing on the front of that person's computer screen. Often this happens inadvertently when people respond to an e-mail and press the **REPLY ALL** button. The next thing you know, everyone knows exactly what you think of your boss or mother-in-law, including your boss or mother-in-law. Yikes!

Reciprocate

Brevity is bliss online. If someone sends you a long e-mail, it's appropriate to acknowledge the effort even if you don't have time to return the favor word for word right away. For instance, if you get a play-by-play account of a friend's vacation, you could simply reply, "Thanks for the update. Great to hear from you. Things are good on this end. Thanks for checking in. Look forward to catching up more."

Listen well

Be sure to read e-mails and message boards before replying and/or posting a message. If you don't look before you leap, you're likely to send or post a reply that is off the mark. In message boards and chat rooms stick to the topic at hand. If you agree with a group e-mail or message board, reply with an informative comment. It's the thought that counts. No one likes to receive dozens of e-mails or read through hundreds of postings that just say "me too."

Don't yell

Using ALL CAPS in chat rooms and message boards is considered poor form. It's the equivalent of YELLING at everyone. It also makes your message more difficult to read. So while it's terrific to relay INFLECTION, make sure you use it sparingly as not to OVER-WHELM people.

One person's junk is another's jewel

Chain letters and junk mail can add up. If you would prefer not to receive chain letters, it's appropriate to send a quick e-mail to the sender saying that while you love staying in touch, you'd prefer not to receive chain letters. Practice what you preach — if you don't like receiving chain letters, don't send them!

Guard personal information

Today's online stranger might be tomorrow's Buddy List pal. But, be smart about giving out personal information online (like your home or work address). It's better to keep those facts to yourself. Etiquette tip: don't ask, don't tell.

Don't forget old friends

While you're meeting new friends online, be sure to remember the old ones. A recent AOL Roper Starch poll indicates more than 40% of people online have connected with someone from their past. The average length of time they'd been out of touch was 12 years! So think back...way back. Then go to AOL Keyword: **Member Profiles** or Keyword: **Online Reunions** to find someone you'd like to get back in touch with.

Curbing junk mail

As for incoming instant messages and e-mails that annoy you, a smart response is to delete them and not write back. Like unsolicited junk mail you receive in your U.S. postal mailbox, junk e-mail can pile up.

For more tips on curbing unwanted e-mail, click on **Mail** on the toolbar and select **Mail Controls** on the pull-down menu.

Members who frequent chat rooms are often more susceptible to receiving junk mail, so consider using a separate screen name for chat.

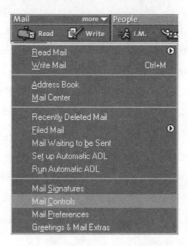

To create a separate screen name go to AOL Keyword: **Screen Name**. Then use mail controls to block all e-mail to this account. This way you'll be free to chat away and unsolicited e-mail won't pile up.

Hi-Wired

AOL *High Speed*
B R O A D B A N D

Do you have the need for speed?

The more you do online, the more you'll likely come to appreciate faster is better. For me, high-speed access is as good as it gets. To find out if you're a candidate for high-speed access, consider some of these benefits:

- Be on AOL and talk on the phone at the same.
- Get the most out of your time online with the fastest Internet connection available and access to cool games, music, movie clips and more.
- Get online instantly with just one click and find what you want online faster.
- No waiting while going from site to site and downloading large files like pictures and music.
- Get high-speed access for about the same price of a second phone line.
- Have another reliable means of connecting with loved ones.

The AOL service offers easy and reliable access for consumers through a variety of platforms - from your phone line to the AOL High-Speed Broadband service for cable, DSL or satellite connections — and AOL 7.0's new design is optimized for any speed, including high-speed Internet connections.

Whenever members sign on to the AOL service using a high-speed connection, special content and programming will automatically appear across the service with instant access to full motion video and high quality audio, including news, sports highlights, movie clips and action games.

AOL High-Speed Broadband features exciting high-speed programming such as:

Movie previews: See the latest trailers for new and upcoming releases on AOL Movie-fone before you go to the theater.

Streaming music and videos: Listen to top artists in digital stereo with the new Radio@AOL and watch the latest hits from pop, rock and hip-hop artists with videos from Rolling Stone and GetMusic.com.

Ongoing news coverage: View breaking news CNN, plus the latest features and headlines from CBS News, weather forecasts from The Weather Channel, entertainment news from E! Online and financial news and analysis from CBS MarketWatch.

Sports coverage: Watch sports news from CNNSI, plus hoops highlights from NBA.com, racing highlights from NASCAR, gridiron action from the NFL and coverage of big sporting events, such as Wimbledon and the NBA Playoffs, from Turner Sports.

Toons, toons and more toons: Watch classic Looney Tunes clips featuring Bugs Bunny, Daffy Duck and the rest of the gang, plus exclusive Web Shorts from Cartoon Network.

Improved game performance: Smoke the dial-up users in your favorite online games with your high-speed connection.

And more! Visit AOL Keyword: **High Speed.**

DAY 2

Get the Info

 I often begin my day by reviewing the AOL Welcome Screen, the weather, news headlines and my horoscope.

By the time I'm through with my morning coffee, I feel connected. That's the beauty of the Internet: You can find what you want, when you want it. The AOL service makes finding the best of the best on the Internet easy.

What can you find?

- Online versions of newspapers and magazines.
- All the information you need to manage your health, finances and daily life.
- Local weather, television and movie listings.
- Up-to-date dictionaries, encyclopedias and atlases.
- From cars to colleges ... you name it, there's something about it online.

By design there are several ways to navigate the AOL service, just as there are several routes from your home to your local grocery store. Don't be surprised when multiple paths take you to the same place.

Sign on

Sign on to the AOL service by double-clicking on the AOL icon 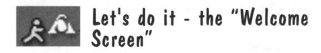 located on your main computer screen (also referred to as your desktop) and then type in your screen name and password in the space provided and clicking on **Sign On.**

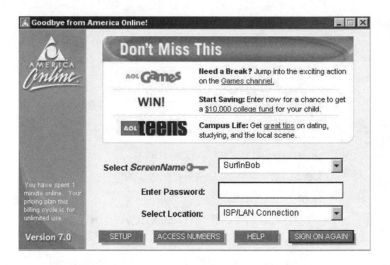

Let's do it - the "Welcome Screen"

As you've already discovered, when you sign on to the AOL service, two windows

come up right away - 1.) the Welcome Screen,
and 2.) the Channel Menu (and your Buddy
List if you set it up on Day 1.)

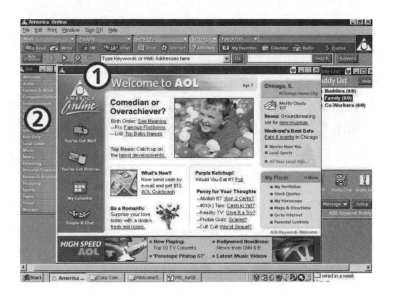

Think of these two together as being like
the lobby of a building — it's a short step from
there to anywhere you want to go.

All of AOL's content offerings are
arranged into categories called "channels."
The Channel Menu appears on the left-hand
side of the screen and is your guide to all of
the content available on the AOL service.
Using your mouse, move the pointer slowly
down the column, without clicking anything.

Click on any one of the channel buttons and you'll go directly to that exclusive AOL online area. No matter what channel you select, you'll quickly find there's lots more behind this screen. Let's look around.

The Channel Menu will stay on your screen whenever you're online, unless you choose to close it by clicking on the **Hide Channels** button. When you're finished looking at a channel, just click on the ☒ in the top right corner of the channel screen.

The other component of the AOL service "lobby" is the Welcome Screen, which will fill most of the space on your screen when you sign on. This is divided into three main sections.

On the left-hand side of the screen are four icons that connect you to popular AOL features described in other sections of this book —You've Got Mail, You've Got Pictures, My Calendar and Chat .

To the right of that section is the biggest part of the Welcome Screen, highlighting some of the most interesting and popular content available on the AOL service that day.

These listings change frequently — several times a day as you sign on and off —so it's worth checking them often.

You'll notice that there are many items in this section that are underlined and in blue letters or even images. Each of these is a "link." Clicking your mouse on a link will connect you to the content described.

When you've finished looking at that page, click the ☒ at the top right corner of it to close the new window and you'll be back at the Welcome Screen.

The far right hand side of the Welcome Screen highlights some of the most popular areas. Click on anything you see and you'll be directly linked to some of AOL's premier features like Maps & Directions, White Pages and Stock Quotes. You'll notice that this area is automatically personalized for you, with local weather, news headlines, and other information for your local area.

You can personalize this column even more by clicking on the **More** link to the right of My Places, then click on the **Change My Places** button. This will allow you to put the AOL service content that's most important to you on the Welcome Screen.

If you're signing on with a high-speed connection, the AOL service will automatically present additional broadband content at the bottom of the Welcome Screen.

There you will be able to click on and view movie trailers, music, videos, news, weather and sports highlights. See page 65 or visit AOL Keyword: **High Speed** for more details.

There are three basic ways to get the information you want on AOL: Keywords, Search and Channels, covered on Day 3.

AOL Keywords

One of the most popular things about the AOL service is the easy-to-use "Keywords" that make it incredibly simple to find your way around online. To get to a particular area on AOL, or to many sites on the Internet, you can just use one word or a simple phrase — such as **"Sports"** or **"News"** instead of a long Web address with lots of "www"s and "colon, backslash, backslash."

If you know the AOL Keyword for the area you want to visit (they are often mentioned in advertisements for various Web sites, new movies, music releases, TV shows, etc. and are included on the bottom of all AOL screens) just follow these three quick steps:

· First, click on the **Keyword** button on the right-hand side of the AOL toolbar. A small "Keyword" box will appear.

· Second, type the word or phrase into the "Enter Word(s)" space in the "Keyword" box.

· Third, click the **Go** button, and you'll be connected to the corresponding area.

Doesn't that sound easy? Try it now with the AOL Keyword: **Wired in a Week**.

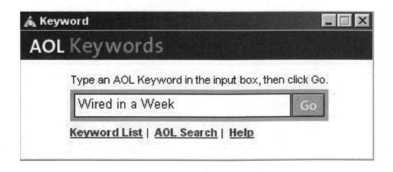

You can ignore spaces and capitalization when you use keywords, so "Wired in a Week" will work as well as "wiredinaweek."

If you don't know the appropriate AOL Keyword, there are a couple of things you can try. First, in the "Keyword" box, next to the "Go" button is a link labeled **"Keyword List."** Click on it to see a full list of thousands of AOL Keywords.

You can also try just entering a word that you think might work as a Keyword. You'll be surprised how often it works. If you're looking for help with your income tax returns, for example, try AOL Keyword: **Taxes**, and you'll find all kinds of help.

If the word or phrase you type isn't recognized as an AOL Keyword, then the system will treat it as a search request (more on those in just a second), so you're one step ahead of the game.

Popular keywords

Here are some of the most popular AOL Keywords:

Auctions	Horoscope	News
Autos	Kids	Pets
Baby	Local	Recipes
Dictionary	Love	Shop
Finance	Maps	Sports
Health	Movies	Taxes
Help	Music	Weather

And, if you can't decide which of the AOL service areas you'd like to visit or just want to experiment, try AOL Keyword: **Explore** and we'll pick for you. Try AOL Keyword: **Keyword** to see today's most popular ten keywords on the service.

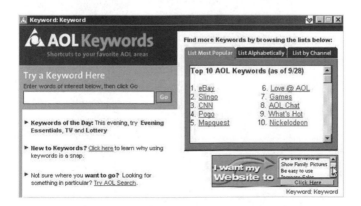

Using AOL search

Sometimes you're trying to find something online in a hurry and you aren't sure where to look for it. If you can't figure out what channel it would be under and you don't know the keyword, does that mean you're out of luck? Not at all. AOL Search is a fast, efficient way to find what you want.

The best way to search is:

Click on the **Search** button on the AOL Toolbar, near the top right corner of your computer screen, or go to AOL Keyword: **Search**.

A new window will open up displaying the AOL Search main screen.

Your cursor will automatically appear in the empty box at the top of the screen. Type what you are looking for and then click on the **Search** button to the right of the search box.

Depending on what you're looking for, it might take a few seconds or more. When the search is complete, you'll see a page with information divided into as many as three categories: Recommended Sites, Matching Categories, and Matching Sites. Not all search requests will produce all three categories. You may also see a list of "sponsored links." These links are provided by a third party and not endorsed by AOL.

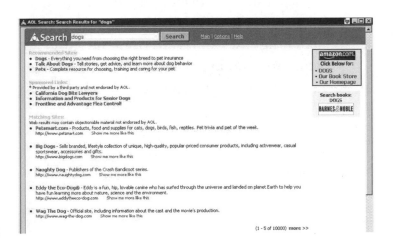

· **Recommended:** These are sites that are most likely to be what you are looking for. Click on the underlined blue text and you'll be connected to a site that should be relevant and helpful.

· **Matching Categories:** This section contains connections to additional lists of sites that may contain relevant information. Click on any of the categories listed to find additional sites.

· **Matching Sites:** This section will list sites that match or come close to matching your search request. The higher up on the list a site is, the more likely it is to be what you're looking for. Note: The matching site results are from the World Wide Web and may contain objectionable material that AOL does not endorse.

When you connect to sites using Search, it's important to know that you won't go back to the Search Results page if you click on the ☒ in the upper right-hand corner of the screen.

Instead, you can go backward using the back arrow button ◁ on your AOL browser toolbar.

To experiment, search for the word "President." One of the options returned to you is the official Web site for the White House, where you can find transcripts of all of the president's statements.

Search for "Lasagna" and find a long list of matching sites with different recipes. An "Australia" search yields all kinds of interesting info.

In addition to the main AOL Search feature, you'll find specific search functions on a lot of the AOL channels, such as Computing and Shopping. These work pretty much the same way, but they search only within that subject area. This can be a convenient tool for finding something in a hurry.

AOL's screen name service

ScreenName 𝕆━━
AOL · Netscape · CompuServe   *Your Key to Unlocking the Best of the Internet*

As you surf and explore different Web sites on the Internet, some sites will ask you to sign in or register. AOL's Screen Name Service makes it easy to visit a range of Web sites using a single name and password — and it's FREE! Instead of trying to remember dozens of different names and passwords, the Screen Name Service helps users register and log into member sites using just one.

Here's how it works ...

When you visit a Web site, just look for the SNS official Sign In button.

ScreenName O━🗝 Sign-In

As an AOL member, you can click on the button to be automatically signed in with your Screen Name. If a new site requires you to register (which many sites do), you can use the information you've already placed in your secure stored profile. You get to choose which pieces of information you want to share with each partner — and which you don't — because protecting your privacy is the highest priority. You can now surf the Web faster and easier - and with fewer hassles.

Visit AOL Keyword: **Screen Name Service** to learn more and to view or update your profile.

The AOL local guide hits close to home

One of the top requests we hear from AOL members is that they want quick and easy access to local content and information. Bottom line: people want to know what's going on in their own backyard. AOL 7.0 prominently features and integrates a wide range of content and city-specific programming from the AOL Local Guide on the Welcome Screen and across channels and sites.

With coverage of more than 30,000 towns in the United States, you can conveniently stay in touch with what's going on in your local community and find the hometown information you want most — from restaurant and movie guides, to news headlines, traffic and weather, entertainment listings, shopping information and much more.

For example, it couldn't be easier to find the right place to dine. Simply type in AOL Keyword: **Local** and select a city. When the main screen for your local guide comes up, type "Dining" in the box in the upper left-hand corner and click on the **GO** button.

Find a number in the yellow pages

Throw out your phone book. Finding the number for a business (or a friend) couldn't be simpler online. On the toolbar, you'll see the word "People."

Click on it and you'll get a pull-down menu and see the words "Yellow Pages" (and "White Pages" as well for people searches). This feature is particularly helpful if you have multiple phone lines and can use your computer and phone at the same time.

Enter either a business category (I picked "Party Supplies" for my trial) or the name of a business you already know.

Enter a nearby town and click on the down arrow to choose the state name. Click on **Find** and a list of related categories will appear to help you refine your search. Each category page provides specific listings with telephone numbers.

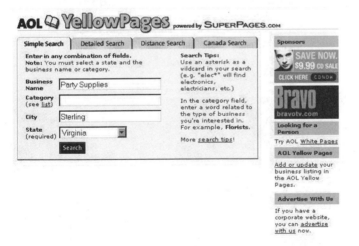

Find a movie

Just enter AOL Keyword: **Movies** and you'll go straight to our Movies area. You can browse recent releases, read reviews, watch trailers and get previews of movies that are coming soon — you can even find out what's hot on video or DVD.

If you're looking for show times or tickets for movies in your area, click on the **Find Local Theaters Near You** link in the center of the screen. This will take you to AOL Moviefone (you can also visit AOL Keyword: **Moviefone**). Type in your city or zip code to find out what's playing at theaters in your hometown. You can also search for movies by title, and then narrow your search by entering your city or zip code. Once you find the movie you want to see, in some cities you can even avoid the long lines at the theatre by purchasing your tickets online.

Whatever you like to do, chances are you'll find something enjoyable when you sign on. From games to music and horoscopes to Hollywood gossip ... there's something for everyone. You may even meet that special someone. Once you get going, having fun online is as easy as turning on the television or shuffling a deck of cards.

Check your horoscope

Checking horoscopes is an online favorite and it couldn't be easier. Even if you don't believe in astrology or take it with a grain of salt, there's something about getting a little bit of tailored advice with a few clicks of the mouse that makes for a fun daily ritual. Just go to AOL Keyword: **Horoscope**.

Gossip

Who can resist taking a few minutes to catch up on who said what to whom, and what they were wearing? The AOL service is a great place to get the latest scoop. Go to AOL Keyword: **Gossip** for up-to-the-minute info from some of the best sources around.

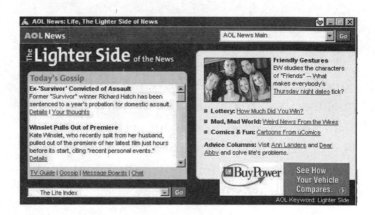

Live celebrity chats

Did you ever imagine that you could sit down with a famous person and ask a few questions? On AOL, you can. Everyday, some of the most powerful, famous, and interesting people in the world come by our AOL Live chat room to take questions from AOL members like you.

Every major candidate in the 2000 presidential election did a chat on AOL Live. So do tons of TV, movie, and recording artists, authors, and other newsmakers. The big chats of the day are often featured on the Welcome Screen. You can also check the full schedule at AOL Keyword: **Live.**

Did you know?

Can you guess the most popular celebrity chat ever on AOL?

    a. Music Legend Madonna
    b. Teen Pop Star Britney Spears
    c. Rapper Eminem
    d. Boy Band *NSYNC

Answer: Britney Spears chatted with more than 234,000 fans, March 1999.

SECRETS DAY 2

· **Get the transcript:** If you miss a scheduled chat, fear not, transcripts are often posted on AOL Live, go to AOL Keyword: **Live**.

· **What's new?** The AOL service is constantly updating and improving its content offerings. Look around when you sign on to see what's new or visit AOL Keyword: **What's New**.

· **STOP!** The AOL logo in the upper right corner of the screen shimmers when a search is underway. If you want to stop a search, click on the **Stop** icon on the toolbar.

· **News you can use:** Use AOL News Profiles instead of searching all over cyberspace for news stories, or worrying that you might miss something of interest; let AOL take care of it. Go to AOL Keyword: **News Profiles** and follow the step-by-step directions so you can receive a daily, tailored news report via e-mail with the information you need and want the most. It's free and it's a great way to stay on top of specific company, sports, medical or local news.

· **Search yourself:** If you're curious about what kind of information is online about you, here's a simple trick: run a search on yourself using the same resources you would use to track down an old friend. See page 151 for more information.

AOL newsletters

You can receive FREE, up-to-date information about your interests, hobbies and more — all delivered directly to your e-mail box.

AOL members can subscribe to newsletters that interest them — with topics available on everything from Health & Fitness, Personal Finance, and Careers to Business Know-How, Sports, Travel and more. Visit AOL Keyword: **Newsletters** to subscribe today.

Hi-Wired

Finding your way around online can make it faster to find your way around offline. My husband never stops to ask for directions, but now he always uses Mapquest to print directions for the fastest route to wherever we're headed.

No more worrying about stopping at a gas station to ask the way. Before you leave, go to AOL Keyword: **Directions** and you'll be brought to Mapquest, where they'll do all the legwork for you. Then just enter the address information for your starting and ending points.

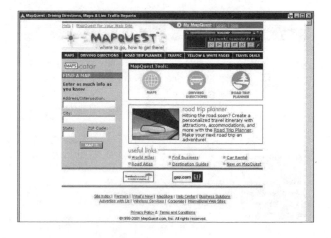

You can choose door-to-door or city-to-city directions, then click on **Get Directions**. You'll get a map and exact, step-by-step printable directions with mileage. Use Mapquest to get directions from the airport or office to your house and save time when guests visit or you are planning a get-together at your home, you can easily pull up, print and forward them by mail or e-mail.

Notes

Welcome
Autos
Careers & Work
Computer Center
Entertainment
Games
Health
House & Home
International
Kids Only
Local Guide
Music
News
Parenting
Personal Finance
Research & Learn
Shopping
Sports
Teens
Travel
Women

DAY 3

Get Around

| Welcome |
| Autos |
| Careers & Work |
| Computer Center |
| Entertainment |
| Games |
| Health |
| House & Home |
| International |
| Kids Only |
| Local Guide |
| Music |
| News |
| Parenting |
| Personal Finance |
| Research & Learn |
| Shopping |
| Sports |
| Teens |
| Travel |
| Women |

We've all heard the expression surfing or searching the Net, but what you really want to do is keep the search part quick and find stuff fast. The AOL Channel lineup is designed to help you do that.

Each channel is set up differently, but they all highlight interesting and up-to-date information and connections to more information on various related topics.

AOL channels include: Autos, Career & Work, Computer Center, Entertainment, Games, Health, House & Home, International, Kids Only, Local Guide, Music, News, Parenting, Personal Finance, Research & Learn, Shopping, Teens, Travel and Women.

Finding information on any of the channels is a simple process — when you see something that looks interesting, click on it and a new window will open up with the information you've asked for. There will probably be other links on the new screen to additional things you might want to explore. When you're done with a particular window, close it by clicking the ☒ in its top right corner.

This is what people mean when they talk about "surfing." It's just clicking on things that look interesting, and seeing where they take you. With AOL, you never have to worry about getting lost. Some of the links you click on will go directly to content created by AOL or one of our partners, others will take you to the World Wide Web.

But it doesn't matter. Just click on the ☒ to close each window when you're done with it, and you'll get back to the main channel menu, or go to AOL Keyword: **Welcome** to get back to the Welcome Screen.

The best way to find out what AOL's exclusive channels offer is to explore. The channel lineup changes periodically to offer members more of what they want, so keep your eyes open for changes and watch for keywords in the bottom right corner of all AOL screens. Spend a few minutes scanning the main pages of each channel.

Here's a quick rundown of the various channels and their top content offerings.

Autos channel: With content from respected sources like Autotrader.com and AutoWeb, you can find the information you need to help you buy or sell your car, compare and contrast different models to find the right fit for you, secure financing, learn proper maintenance and care for your vehicle and even find the dealer nearest you.

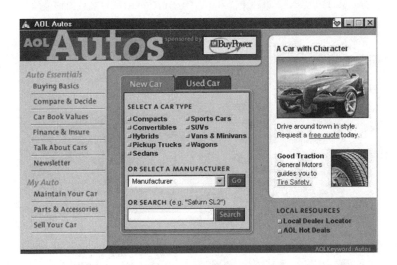

Whether you're looking for a new or used car, a Nissan or a Cadillac, a coupe or a convertible, you can find it here. And if you're an auto enthusiast, you'll find articles, message

boards, libraries, and guides on how to jump-
start a car, change a flat, and even parallel
park. Use AOL Keyword: **Autos**.

Careers & Work channel: The Careers &
Work channel (featuring Monster.com) is a
great place to turn for information on finding
a job, starting a business or improving your
career. You can search hundreds of thousands
of job listings, submit your resume online, or
have jobs e-mailed to you as they become
available. You can also check your MyMon-
ster account directly from the channel to see
how many employers have viewed your
resume.

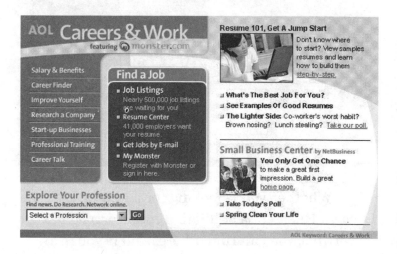

The channel also provides great resume writing and interviewing advice, as well as a Salary Calculator (provided by Salary.com) that let's you check median salaries for your occupation in your area. The first rung on the ladder begins at AOL Keyword: **Careers & Work**.

Computer Center channel: No channel lineup on AOL would be complete without a channel dedicated to computing. The Computer Center channel offers virtually everything you need to know to make your computer hum.

Founded on a very basic truth: If you're using the AOL service, you're using a computer, and the more you know about your computer, the more you'll get out of your AOL experience. Visit AOL Keyword: **Computer Center**. If you learn of computer viruses, this is a good place to track down the latest virus protection updates you can always go to AOL Keyword: **AntiVirus** as well.

Entertainment channel: An up-to-the minute source for information on the latest, most talked-about movies, TV shows, music and books.

The Entertainment channel gives you a variety of ways to keep track of your favorite celebrities and all of the entertainment news from sources such as E! Online, Entertainment Weekly, TV Guide, MTV, People and more. AOL Keyword: **Entertainment**.

Games channel: The AOL Games channel (powered by EA.com), as you might guess from its name, is another prime source of online fun. You can play everything from simple card games to complex sci-fi action games. AOL Keyword: **Games**.

You should be aware that there is a premium charge for some games. It's also worth noting that the Games channel displays ratings providing information about both the age-appropriateness and content of each game. One of the most popular games is Slingo, a combination of bingo and a slot machine. Visit AOL Keyword: **Slingo**.

Health channel: Nothing is more important than your health, and this channel gives you all the information, tips and tools you need to have more control over your own well-being. Get the health content you want quickly and easily from the most respected sources in the industry, including WebMD, Thrive Online, iVillage and CBS HealthWatch.

You can also research health questions, communicate with health care professionals, participate in chat rooms and message boards about a variety of health-related issues and even order prescriptions online. Visit AOL Keyword: **Health**.

Smart tips for using the Internet for health information

· Trust in a name — there are thousands of health sites out there, make sure you know the source of information. AOL's health partners all meet stringent criteria, so you don't have to worry about reading the fine print from web site to web site. Many medical schools and centers also have reputable sites.

· Use common sense and know when to talk to the doctor — the Internet is not a substitute for clinical care.

· Leverage the online community — it's estimated one in four people who go online for health information also joins support groups. Many sites offer chat rooms and message boards where people can talk and share their experiences with kindred spirits — which can sometimes be healing in itself.

House & Home channel: The House & Home channel (featuring Homestore.com), offers tips, advice, and information on gardening, home improvement and decorating. It also connects you to the world's largest collection of online real estate listings. Whether you're looking to buy or rent, for new construction or a fixer-upper, check out the real estate listings on this popular channel. Many listings now include 3-D virtual interior and exterior home tours. My husband and I found our home online and have also pursued mortgages online. For more information on online real estate see page 186.

This channel also can help you add style and comfort to any home, however modest or grand. The key to a comfortable, relaxing home is under the doormat at AOL Keyword: **Home.**

International channel: Whether you're an armchair traveler, an avid globetrotter or somewhere in between, AOL's International channel gives you the world. Traveling overseas? Turn to AOL Keyword: **International** for all you want to know about your destination including maps, cultural and political information, a currency converter and a time zone tool. Foreign newspapers are also available, as well as message boards and chats in foreign languages.

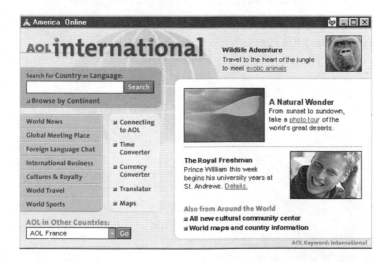

And you can use the channel's translation tool in advance of your trip to learn useful words and phrases. Curious about the AOL service in other countries? Check out the box in the lower left hand corner "AOL in Other Countries" to explore AOL in the UK, Japan, Australia, etc.

Kids Only channel: As the sign says, this is a channel for kids only. The entire channel is geared toward children ages 6-12 with age appropriate content that gives kids the resources they want and parents the peace of mind they need. Kids can explore content from Nickelodeon, Cartoon Network, TIME for Kids, Sports Illustrated for Kids, Fox Kids, KidoNet, KidsWB, Sesame Street and much more. This channel also features a "Kids Only Jr." area for children ages 2-5. AOL Keyword: **Kids Only.**

Local Guide channel: The AOL Local Guide provides AOL members with locally relevant news, community resources, entertainment, and commerce in an engaging, easy-to-use format.

The Local Guide covers more than 30,000 cities, towns and neighborhoods across the U.S., and partners with some of the nation's top local media companies to deliver branded local news, weather, sports, traffic and entertainment. Visit AOL Keyword: **Local**.

Music channel: It's easy to discover and experience music on the AOL Music channel, AOL Keyword: **Music**. Listen to the radio or CDs, download music or watch videos. With great content from major and independent record labels, Digital Club Network, HBO, Rollingstone.com, CDNOW, TNT, MusicNet, CNN Worldbeat and National Public Radio, you can find information about your favorite artists and purchase the latest music all in one place.

News channel. AOL's News channel, the #1 destination for news and information in cyberspace, features continuously updated news stories each day from a variety of leading news providers, including Reuters, Associated Press, NPR, the New York Times, Time, CNN and CBS.

AOL News has become a national sounding board for conversation and a hub for current event debates and discussions. AOL members aren't just up-to-date on the news, they're part of it. AOL Keyword: **News.**

Parenting channel: The AOL Parenting channel provides resources for busy parents looking for advice, support and tips for enriching their family life. Explore content from iVillage, Oxygen, Parenting.com, Sesame Workshops, drSpock.com, and much more. The Parenting channel also features one of the most comprehensive pregnancy guides on the Web, helping expectant parents make decisions and seek advice during this life stage. Visit AOL Keyword: **Parenting.**

Testimonial: "Pregnant? You'll find informa-tion and support in AOL's Mom-to-Mom Commu-nity."

When Jo Parker learned she was pregnant, she joined the March 2001 Pregnancy Circle in AOL's Mom-to-Mom community. There she met other women whose babies were due around the same time.

They gathered to express worries, exchange the latest information and get support from one another. When Jo was assigned to bed rest, her husband strung a telephone line across the ceiling of the living room and connected it to a laptop so she wouldn't miss anything.

Jo came to depend on these women not only for advice but also for the support, friendship, and companionship she needed to get through the dif-ficult period.

Today, she remembers fondly, "You really get attached to everyone, I have a network of over 100 people to turn to." Pregnancy Circles, available 24 hours a day, in due course become Baby Circles and the bonds endure. Visit AOL Keyword: **Preg-nancy Circles** for more information.

Personal Finance channel: Personal Finance gives you the tools to track stocks, research companies, and follow your own portfolio. It also provides tools to help you pay your bills, track your household budget, and calculate your taxes. AOL Keyword: **Personal Finance.**

For all of your online banking and investing needs, you don't need to look any further than AOL's Personal Finance channel — with big industry leaders like Citigroup, Schwab, and CFSB Direct all under one roof. And if you're looking for information on investment strategies, financial planning or market commentary — you'll find sources including CBS-MarketWatch, TheStreet.com, Fool.com, Money.com, CNNfn, and SmartMoney.

This channel is for the homeowner, the stockholder, and the just-plain-everyday person who strives to put his or her life and finances in order, and for all of us who want to make the most of our economic resources.

Research & Learn channel: Whether you need general reference resources, help with schoolwork, college admissions, enhancing your child's education, or furthering your own professional education, the AOL Research & Learn channel is a great place to turn for content from PBS, National Geographic and World Book.

You can even earn a college degree and pursue career enhancing course work and hobbies of all kinds through AOL's new online campus area with partners like the University of Phoenix at AOL Keyword: **Research.**

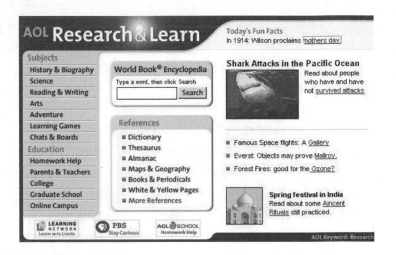

Research & Learn also offers a handy collection of desktop references. You can find the *Merriam-Webster's Collegiate Dictionary* (AOL Keyword: **Collegiate**) and *The Merriam-Webster Thesaurus* (AOL Keyword: **Thesaurus**).

Shopping channel: The Shop@AOL channel is AOL's equivalent of a major marketplace, complete with large department stores, specialty shops, outlet stores and even grocery stores. Best of all, they're open 24 hours a day, 7 days a week. To reach the Shop@AOL channel, go to AOL Keyword: **Shopping**. A complete rundown of online shopping is covered on Day 5.

Sports channel: Get the latest sports stories, stats, scores, lineups and more. You can follow any professional sports team, participate in fantasy sports leagues and much more on the best sports site around. AOL Keyword: **Sports**, features CBS Sportsline, NFL.com, NBA.com, NASCAR.com and CNN/SI, all under one roof on the AOL Sports channel.

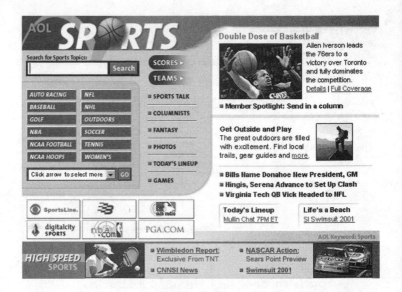

Fantasy sports

One of the fastest growing hobbies among sports fans is online fantasy sports leagues. At the beginning of the real-life baseball, football, basketball, or whatever season, people choose their favorite players and pick teams.

As the season goes on, they follow how those players do, and get points based on different statistics (home runs in baseball, points in basketball, touchdowns in football, etc.). How well selected players perform, determines who wins the game.

AOL makes playing in fantasy leagues easy. You can check in every day for updates about how your team and your opponents' teams are doing. You can also get all kinds of advice from sports experts.

Different sports will work differently, but visit AOL Keyword: **Fantasy Sports** in the months before your favorite sports season starts for more information on how to get started.

Teens channel: Teenagers have their own hangout at the Teens channel, a collection of news, entertainment, fashion and friends.

Features include Teen People (an online version of the magazine), a forum just for teen girls, and links to teen-related areas throughout the AOL service. Of particular interest are the teen chat rooms and message boards. Catch a wave to the Teens channel at AOL Keyword: **Teens**.

Travel channel: It's a destination designed for travelers, whether your trip is for business or pleasure.

Everything you need to plan the perfect and most cost-effective trip is gathered in the Travel channel, powered by Travelocity, from information on vacation resorts and exotic ports to traveler reports and news of all sorts at AOL Keyword: **Travel**.

Women's channel: Not enough hours in the day? Head straight to the Women's channel where everything you need to keep in touch and up-to-date is just a click away. Explore content from Oxygen, Women.com, Oprah.com, iVilliage and much more.

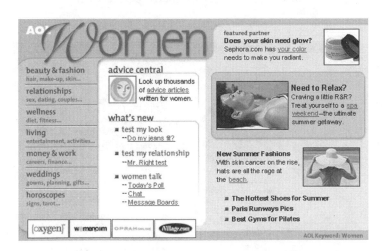

In the Women's channel you'll find the latest beauty and fashion news, relationship advice, diet and fitness tips, career counsel and a strong community of women always willing to provide guidance and feedback at AOL Keyword: **Women.**

AOL Latino

AOL has brought together great content from around the world to offer AOL Latino, a new channel on the AOL service providing a unique array of Spanish and English language content and community features.

AOL Latino connects members of the AOL Latin American services in Argentina, Brazil and Mexico with the rapidly growing community of Hispanic AOL members in the U.S., providing enhanced communication and helping to create new and vibrant online communities. Visit AOL Keyword: **Latino** to access the news, entertainment and community features you want in English and Spanish and explore content from People en Espanol, Hispanic Business, Super Onda, EFE, Gusto Magazine and much, much more.

SECRETS DAY 3

Customizing your AOL toolbar

If there are AOL screens or Web sites that you go to frequently, you can add them to your AOL Toolbar. Simply drag the favorite place heart 🫀 icon from your AOL screen or the Web site to the right side of your AOL Toolbar and let go.

Follow the onscreen directions to choose your custom icon and label. To remove one of the pre-populated icons such as Quotes, Perks and Calendar, right-click on the icon and choose Remove from Toolbar.

Wired Secret from Carrie in AOL Member Services, Ogden, UT. — Keyboard shortcuts that save time!

Here are some great keyboard shortcuts. Hold down the Control (Ctrl) key on your keyboard while pressing the corresponding key

Ctrl R = read your mail
Ctrl K = access keywords
Ctrl M = write an e-mail
Ctrl L = locate a member
Ctrl G = get a profile
Ctrl I = send an IM
Ctrl P = print
Ctrl O = open a file
Ctrl Y = add to My Calendar
Ctrl S = save a file
Ctrl F = find in the top window
Ctrl N = create a new text document

When typing e-mail or IMs

Ctrl B = bold
Ctrl U = underline
Ctrl T = italicize
Ctrl A = to highlight all text
Ctrl C = copy
Ctrl X = to cut
Ctrl V = paste
Ctrl Z = to undo

Don't miss great member exclusives

You won't want to miss special member exclusives in the Music, Entertainment and other channels. Special promotions include concert tickets and walk-ons on some of television's hottest shows. Just to name a few:

- AOL members had first crack at tickets for Madonna's Drowned Tour when she came to the United States.

- AOL members also got the jump on Britney Spears concert tickets for her Fall 2001 concert tour.

· AOL members and fans of the hit series "The West Wing" had the chance to win a trip to Hollywood, go behind-the-scenes of the award-winning show and "do lunch" with a cast member.

· AOL members had the opportunity to weigh in on naming Mimi's baby on the Drew Carey Show.

Make your vote count with AOL polls

Online polls are forever changing the way we interact with the news and what's going on — and now you can be a big part of it. Polls give you a voice and an opportunity to weigh in on anything — from presidential politics to the break-up of Tom and Nicole.

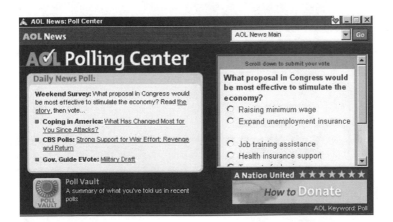

On AOL, polls are some of the most popular features among members and they are a great way to take the real-time pulse of America. Twelve people vote in an AOL poll every second and at any given time there are about 500 polls on the AOL service for you to participate in. Votes are tallied anonymously and give you a chance to see how your opinions stack up against other members.

Look for polls throughout the AOL service on a wide variety of topics. You can always find the 'Daily News Poll' at Keyword: **Poll**, and every week the results of most popular polls on AOL can be found at Keyword: **Poll Vault**.

Hi-Wired

Radio@AOL turns your computer into a stereo - offering 75 channels in all music genres, as well as celebrity-programmed channels, holiday features, news and more. To tune in, simply click on the **Radio** icon at the top of the new AOL Toolbar, or visit AOL Keyword: **Radio.**

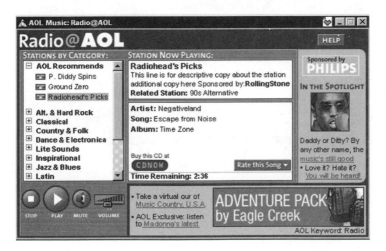

Interested in finding the hottest new and up-and-coming acts in music? Check out AOL's Artist Discovery Network and be the first to discover the best of online music and more.

Want to know what artists are playing in your area? Type in your zip code to find out who's playing where you live or in other areas of the country. AOL Keyword: **Artist Discovery Network.**

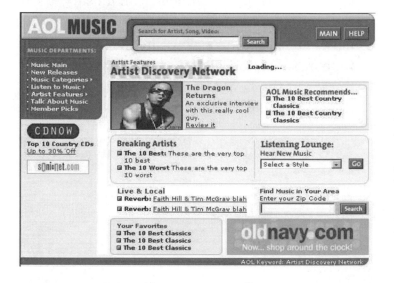

DAY 4

Get a Life

 Kids grow up so fast — everybody always wants to see the latest pictures. If my parents could see new pictures of my daughter and sons every day, they'd be thrilled (and would still want more!).

Now, viewing and sharing your photos online is just a click away. "You've Got Pictures," the online photo service for AOL members, works with both film and digital cameras. Once your pictures are online, you can organize them into fun albums with background colors and captions. Then instantly share those special moments with any of your family and friends who have an e-mail address.

Traditional film users

It's easy to turn your film into online pictures you can share. Look for the AOL logo on the film-processing envelope at a participating retailer. Fill in your AOL e-mail address, and in a few days when you sign on you'll hear a new announcement, "Welcome, You've Got Pictures!"

To see how they turned out, click on the
You've Got Pictures icon  on the Welcome
Screen, then click **View** and use the scroll bar
on the right-hand side of the screen to check
out all of the pictures.

World's Best Dog

Next Picture ▶

If you like what you see, you can either
send a single picture to anyone online in an e-
mail, or create an album with multiple pictures to share.

Digital camera users

If you have a digital camera or scanner, you can also upload photos to the "You've Got Pictures" service. Using the multiple picture upload tool, digital camera and scanner you can enjoy the benefits of free unlimited storage for your digital images and can order real photo prints of your favorites at the Kodak Photo Store.

Here are the steps:

· **Step 1** Click on the **You've Got Pictures** logo from the AOL Welcome Screen.

· **Step 2** Click on the **Upload Pictures** button.

AOL members get free storage space for photos.

· **Step 3** Type in a name for your album. You can upload to an existing album or create a new one.

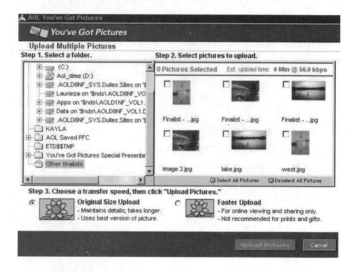

· **Step 4** Click on the upload tool. You can upload multiple pictures at once or a single picture at a time.

· **Step 5** Click on the **Browse** button to view thumbnails of your images and locate your photo.

· **Step 6** Click on the **Upload Picture** button. Your photo is now stored online.

You can customize your photo album by adding a title, captioning your photos, and choosing a background, color and layout. Go to AOL Keyword: **Pictures** for more information and explore how fun and easy photo sharing can be.

Having fun with digital photography

More amateur photographers than ever before are turning to digital camera and the Internet to process their memories.

Advantages of digital cameras include:

Instant gratification

You can see the photo right then and there. There's no waiting for the development process. You can literally take pictures of the kids Christmas morning and e-mail them to friends and family around the world before noon. I know people who have their wedding pictures sent to them while they're honeymooning, because they just can't wait to see them.

Sharing

Traditionally, a lot of people get "double" prints so they can send copies to friends and family. With digital photos you can send them to as many people as you want, anywhere in the world. And you can easily order reprints, so there's real value there. You can even create online albums and share those.

Saves on film & development costs

You don't have to use film (pictures are stored inside your camera and downloaded to your computer). With a color printer you have the option of printing only the pictures you want — this can be a real money saver over time. On a roll of 24, most people — on a good day — get about 6-7 photos they really like and consider "keepers" while the rest end up in a shoebox, so this is a lot more efficient. And if you like to frame 5x7 prints and keep wallet size photos — digital photography is made to order since you can easily and affordably customize the size of the prints you want.

Touch ups

As you get a little more advanced, there is software to help you crop, tweak, remove "red eye," touch up, brighten, move and manipulate images. Often this is built into software that comes with the cameras or printers.

Safeguards images

Storing photos on the Web safeguards against one of everyone's worst nightmares — losing your photos or having them damaged in a fire, flood, etc. If they are on the Web, even if your computer melts or is destroyed, they'll still be there because they're hosted on a server somewhere else. This is so valuable, many people are digitizing existing images — old family photos, baby and wedding pictures — just in case. And insurance companies advise taking pictures of your property and belongings and storing them online too.

Love@AOL

Finding love online is fun and easy, and it works! Love@AOL debuted in 1996 as a Valentine's Day programming special on the AOL service. In the first year, personals grew to 12,000.

Since then, personals have exploded to nearly one million. America Online gets nearly 250 letters every month from couples who have found love online and we estimate upwards of 10,000 marriages have been sparked by people who have met on the AOL service.

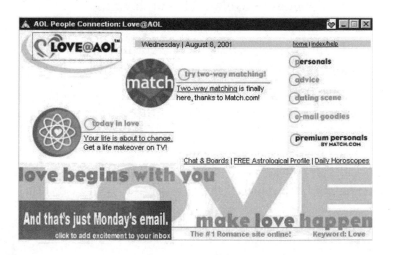

It's no wonder "digital dating" has gone mainstream. Every day on Love@AOL (AOL Keyword: **Love**) thousands of people who might not otherwise have met — maybe because they don't live near each other or "don't get out enough" — meet and communicate online.

Love@AOL provides the perfect forum to mingle and get to know people at your own convenience and pace, and features one of the largest collections of photo personals anywhere in cyberspace. Match.com is the premier provider of personals to Love@AOL.

They're easy to browse. If you'd like to create your own personal, just follow the directions. It takes a matter of minutes, but remember; the information is public, so don't post personal information like your home address or telephone number.

 **Testimonial: Renee met Derrick in a Christian Romance chat room on AOL and chatted with him for a few days before telling him that she knew the perfect woman for him — her friend Charlotte.**

Renee put Derrick and Charlotte in touch, and the two hit it off instantly — Renee was right, they were well suited for each other. They exchanged e-mails and instant messages for a few months before meeting, and when they met the sparks flew. They would correspond for several more months before Derrick moved to Atlanta to be with Charlotte and get married.

Communities on AOL

Community and communication are the hallmarks of the AOL service. Each week AOL members spend approximately 10 million hours chatting and hundreds of thousands of messages are posted every day on AOL's message boards.

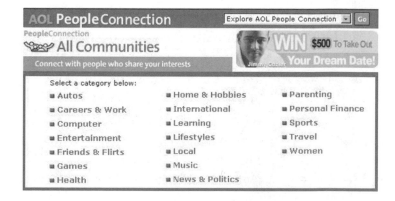

From chats, instant messaging and message boards, to member home pages — AOL's community tools help members stay in touch and foster new relationships.

To start connecting with others who share your interests, visit AOL's People Connection, where you will find links to all of the AOL Community Centers. AOL offers all of the community tools on the community centers to help members stay in touch — chats, message boards, and home pages — all focused on particular topics.

Groups@AOL

Every minute a new person joins a group within the popular Groups@AOL feature. Imagine a place where you can join friends and family to talk and share news — no matter where you're located in the county or around the world.

With Groups@AOL you can plan parties, share family photos and even chat in private. It's also a great place for soccer moms to come together online and share schedules, photos or even use the shared calendar to arrange the next carpool.

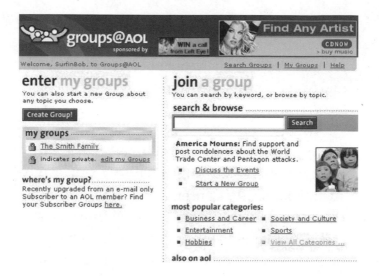

You can make your group completely private, which gives you the choice not only of what information you share, but whom you share it with. To create a Group, visit AOL Keyword: **Groups** and click on the **Create Group** button, then follow the easy, on-screen, step-by-step instructions.

Note: Your group can be "private" for gatherings of family and friends, or "public" for meeting new people who share your interests. Decide which type of Group you want to create.

· **Step 1** Choose a name for your group.
· **Step 2** Choose a title for your group's
         main page.
· **Step 3** Choose a style for your group.
· **Step 4** Create your member profile.

Your Group is now complete. You can now
start to invite friends and family to join in
the fun!

If you have questions or want to learn
some great tips for using Groups @AOL,
there's a special area called the "Founder's
Forum" (AOL Keyword: **Founder's Forum**),
where you can go to ask questions of AOL's

Community Leaders and share tips with
other Group founders.

**Testimonial: AOL Can Help
You Connect with Long-Lost
Pals and Classmates in Just
Seconds**

After graduating from college in 1987, Virginia
Hume Onufer moved to Boston to start a new job
and a new life.

Having little time to visit with her college
friends, Virginia eventually lost touch with almost
all of them. More than a decade later, now married
and a mother, Virginia wanted to re-connect with
her old friends. She used AOL to start the search —
and found that many were AOL members.

After swapping e-mails and instant messages
with them, she decided to set up an AOL Group
(AOL Keyword: **Groups**) so everyone could connect
at the same time.

Now she and her friends communicate daily.
They even use the Group page to post pictures of
their children and spouses, along with old shots
from their college days.

Virginia feels engaged in her friends' lives in a way she hasn't since college. They had so much fun re-connecting that they recently got together for a face-to-face reunion — planned online, of course.

Looking for an old friend?

Have you ever wondered whatever happened to your prom date? How about the classmates you promised to stay in touch with, but didn't? You can be back in touch in just minutes with "online reunion" sites. A great place to start is **Classmates.com**.

After filling out information on which school you attended or military unit you belonged to, you can view lists of people who studied or served with you. From there, you can contact people via e-mail, message board, etc. and even post past and current photos. There are some fees attached.

Greeting cards

Online greeting cards are an easy and creative way to let someone know they are in your thoughts. From birthday greetings to inspirational messages to "just because" notes, you can say everything online.

At AOL Keyword: **Greetings** you'll find an enormous variety of cards offered by AmericanGreetings.com, many with music and animation. Select the type of card you want to send, click on it, and then follow the steps to make it your own personal greeting.

Throw a party with AOL invitations!

AOL Invitations makes organizing get-togethers fun and easy. They allow you to create a personalized online invitation and send it to friends and family; guests can then RSVP, add the event to AOL My Calendar (reviewed on page 195), find directions and see who else is coming — all in one place at AOL Keyword: **Invitations.**

Can't make up your mind? Try AOL decision guides

AOL's decision guides can help you with a number of life's important decisions — from finding the perfect pet to selecting the car that fits your lifestyle or the city that is right for you. Decision guides can even help you with important career moves or in determining which hairstyle best suits you. Decision guides can be found throughout the service on a wide array of topics.

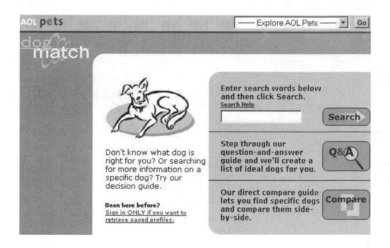

Online search for a furry friend

 There are more than 25,000 animals available online, and the Internet can be a blessing for pet owners and pets. Many shelters estimate the Internet plays a role in about 50 percent of their adoptions and that these tend to be more successful, with fewer pets returned.

There are a lot of online resources to help people make informed choices so they know which pet is best for them and what to expect. This is critical, especially around the holidays when many pets are adopted and given as gifts.

Many come back to shelters weeks later when people realize they didn't quite understand the commitment involved in having a pet.

Offering a pet adoption gift certificate can be a good alternative to presenting a live animal. This way the recipient will make the choice, which experts say is important because it's such a personal decision.

Online personal-decision guides can help the prospective owner discern which pet is best. They can help you identify the pet that best fits your lifestyle by posing some key questions about travel schedule, personal space and whether you have children. For example, you might think you want a horse, only to find out you're really a candidate for a fish.

SECRETS DAY 4

· **Looking for an excuse to send an e-mail greeting to a friend?** Checkout AOL Keyword: **Greetings** to find a monthly list of Coming Events near the bottom of the page. Turns out that August 6-12 is National Smile Week. Who Knew? Every holiday, light-hearted or serious — can be found here, and gives you a reason for getting in touch.

· **Lookin' for love:** Based on AOL member feedback, photo personals are generally more effective than those without, so it's worth taking time to include a picture if you can. Step-by-step instructions are posted on Love @AOL (AOL Keyword: **Love.**)

· **R.S.V.P:** Even if you don't use online invitations, consider providing an e-mail address for R.S.V.P's. It's often a more convenient way for guests to respond and it keeps your phone from ringing off the hook.

Digital cameras: A lot of people ask me what digital camera or videocamera they should get and if it's a good time to buy one. Here are two general rules of thumb: First, stick with the big brand names — Kodak, Sony, etc., as they are most likely to be compatible with any other equipment you have or may acquire down the road. Second, ask yourself if you'll derive real value from the product now. If you will, then go for it. Don't overbuy. I generally advise people to walk before you run — purchase a mid-range/mid price model. You can always add on or upgrade over time.

Online dating dos and don'ts

You've met a great guy (or gal) online and you've shared your life stories, your innermost secrets, your dreams, and you've even traded pictures from grade school through college and even a picture of you in your high school band uniform (which you wouldn't show just anybody).

Now you're ready to take your online romance offline and into the real world. Here's some pointers for making your first in-person meeting safe and successful:

- **DO** schedule the first meeting as a double date, or take a few friends along for a group outing.

· **DON'T** allow your date to pick you up at your home or office.

· **DO** safeguard your home address and all other personal information.

· **DON'T** plan to stay overnight with your date, or allow him/her to make your travel arrangements.

· **DO** meet in a well-lighted public place where there is a lot of activity.

· **DON'T** plan a full day outing. Meet for coffee or a drink on the first date to give your offline relationship time to develop — in much the same way as your online romance did.

· **DON'T** feel obligated to finish your date or agree to go on another. Answer honestly if you are asked out again.

· **DO** pay attention to details and listen to your intuition — your dates' actions, your surroundings, and your feelings. If you feel at all uncomfortable, or notice any strange or unusual signs, excuse yourself politely and say good-bye.

Hi -Wired

AOL 🏠 Hometown

Create a Web page

AOL Hometown is the place where millions of AOL members create and share their personal home pages with friends, family and others with similar interests, hobbies and backgrounds. Anyone on the Web can locate and browse these home pages all in one convenient place at hometown.aol.com.

AOL Hometown is organized into several categories where AOL members can list their home pages, so they can be found quickly and easily.

AOL's 1-2-3 Publish is an easy to use tool to help you create and publish a home page on the Web. Once you're ready to take your home page to the next level with more functionality and creativity you can use AOL's Easy Designer tool.

Tell your story to others: adding a personal page to AOL Hometown allows you to express yourself by sharing more information with people you meet online. You can display photos, talk about hobbies and discuss aspirations.

Other popular ways to use private and public home pages include: introducing a new baby; bragging about your cat or dog with a pet home page; featuring a band with a music home page; and displaying wedding pictures online with a photo home page. For more information visit AOL Keyword: **Hometown**.

Notes

DAY 5

Get the Goods

If you love to shop, you'll soon come to agree the Internet is the best invention since the mall. Once you get a taste of how easy Shop@AOL is, you'll come back again and again.

You can shop any time of day or night from the comfort of your home or while you're at work. You can even shop in your pajamas!

And because AOL has millions of members, we're able to use that buying power to negotiate some of the best deals in cyberspace — or anywhere else. According to the U.S. Department of Commerce, over $300 billion in business will be conducted over the Internet during the first decade of the new millennium. Chances are good that you'll be one of those people making a purchase online soon, if you haven't already.

What is Shop@AOL?

Shopping is one of the fastest-growing online activities. Take a look at just a few of the advantages of Shop@AOL:

· You'll never have to "fight the crowds" at the mall, find a parking space or worry about getting a last minute gift.

· Shop@AOL has a huge selection of high-quality products and great values, so good that experts have called Shop@AOL the "Internet's Miracle Mile," after Chicago's famous shopping district.

· There's no more dragging packages from the store to the car, and from the car into the house. Products ordered online are delivered right to your doorstep, or wherever else you'd like. Shipping options also make online shopping ideal for gift giving.

· Shop@AOL makes it incredibly easy to find what you're looking for — search by item, merchant and/or price, making comparison-shopping a breeze.

It doesn't matter whether you're buying a frying pan for $15 or a video camera for $1,500 — Shop@AOL is made to order. Apparel, jewelry, home furnishings, gourmet foods, toys, books, cosmetics, flowers — you name it, it's available online.

If you're making a major purchase like a house, car, furniture or appliance — or if you're deciding which car seat to buy for your new baby — you can save a lot of research time and make informed choices by starting your search online. You'll be amazed at all the useful consumer information you can find. It's no wonder people in the market for new homes and cars are signing on in record numbers.

AOL's certified merchant guarantee

We want to make sure that your shopping experience is everything you thought it would be. To ensure this, all AOL Certified Merchants must meet our high standards for customer service, secure transactions, and privacy protection before they sell a single item. And on top of that, their return policy is backed up by AOL's money-back guarantee.

AOL guarantees your total shopping satisfaction. Visit AOL Keyword: **Guarantee** for complete details.

 **Our promise to you**

If you're not satisfied with your purchase for any reason, please visit the store's customer service area for instructions on how to resolve your issue. If you still don't get a resolution consistent with the store's posted customer service policies, outline your complaint and contact Shopping Help at AOL Keyword: **Shopping Help.** We'll look over the details and intervene on your behalf to make sure you get a satisfactory response.

AOL protects you

Every time you shop with any of AOL's Certified Merchants, you are protected against liability in the unlikely event of credit card fraud; simply follow your credit card company's reporting procedure. AOL will reimburse you up to $50 for any remaining liability for unauthorized charges.

AOL offers a level of safety and security not available at your local mall. Since the creation of AOL's shopping area and the inception of our Guarantee in October 1996, the Shopping channel has never received a report of a credit card that was compromised during a shopping transaction with Certified Merchants on AOL.

Our commitment to our members is to maintain this record by providing you with advanced, up-to-date security technology.

Security

How does AOL make shopping online so safe? AOL helps protect you from transaction fraud by making sure all AOL merchants provide a secure and safe environment for credit card purchases.

When you make a purchase through the AOL service, the information you provide is scrambled. As a result, in the highly unlikely event that an unauthorized person intercepts the transmission, he/she won't be able to read or to understand any of your personal information.

For your convenience and safety, AOL automatically provides you with built-in scrambling technology (known as a secure browser) if you are using AOL 7.0, 6.0, or 5.0. For others, there's more information about upgrading your browser at AOL Keyword: **Browser.**

Official AOL Mail

Protect yourself from credit card fraud by following this simple guideline: NEVER give your credit card information or password to unauthorized persons contacting you via e-mail or instant message, however clever or compelling they may sound.

For tips on identifying official AOL Mail, go to AOL Keyword: **Official AOL Mail**.

 ## Let's do it - Shop@AOL

Some people would like to shop online, but they just don't know where to start. On AOL, that's not a problem. Use the Channel Menu to go to the Shopping channel — the entrance into AOL's online mall. Click on the **Shop** icon on the AOL toolbar, or enter AOL Keyword: **Shopping**, and there you are. You'll see that AOL has done all the legwork. We've pulled together the best of the best to create an amazing one-stop shopping destination — Shop@AOL.

The Shop@AOL main page is where you'll find featured specials, departments, search, clearance center, luxury, gift areas and an A to Z Store Directory. If you know what you're looking for, there's an easy way to find it.

Shop@AOL's search feature helps you find just the right item. This feature can be found in the center of the Shop@AOL main screen.

It works the same way as the regular AOL search tool, except that the results you get will be a selection of items from our shopping partners that match word you entered. Give it a try with "sweater" as an example.

Once you've found the product you want, it's time to try making a purchase at one of our certified merchants. Each of our merchant sites works slightly differently, but they all follow the same basic principles. Just follow these easy steps:

· When the item you want to purchase is on your screen, look for a button that says "Add to shopping cart," "Purchase," or something similar. Click on it.

Buy it Now!

Add this item to your shopping cart.
You can always remove it later.

· Your shopping cart will display the item you've selected. You can either go back to shopping for other items to add to your cart or click **Proceed to checkout.**

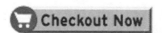

· You'll then be presented with a form to
  fill out, asking for your name, shipping
  address and other information, along
  with your credit card number. All of the
  participating merchants on Shop@AOL
  have met stringent criteria and use
  cutting-edge security technology.

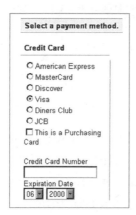

· If you're buying an item to send as a gift,
  you'll also be able to enter the appropriate
  name and address and even text to have
  printed on a gift card.

· You will be given a last chance to change
  your choices or decide not to make the
  purchase. If you want to go ahead, click
  OK or **YES**.

Please be sure to click this button.

· Your credit card will be charged, and the product will delivered to your house or to the recipient of your gift. The site will e-mail you a confirmation notice/receipt. It's a good idea to print this out and save it until the product arrives.

Procrastinate without guilt - last minute gifts

If you're among the 40% of Americans who wait until the last minute to shop for the holidays, for birthdays or for other special occasions, fear not. Shop@AOL's "Last Minute Gifts" specialty shop highlights a selection of popular, brand-name merchandise from dozens of AOL merchants, with all gifts guaranteed to arrive within 24 to 48 hours after a purchase is made.

Online gift certificates are also a great last minute option and can be e-mailed around the world in a matter of minutes. They can be sent Christmas morning and arrive Christmas Day — they're real lifesaver in the holiday homestretch. Visit AOL Keyword: **Last Minute.**

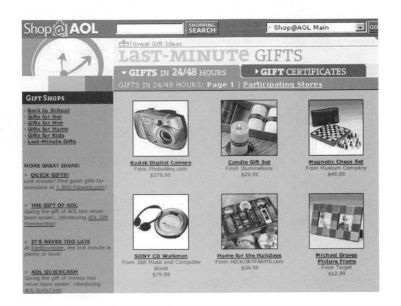

Be a bargain bug

AOL pulls together the top deals. Visit AOL Keyword: **Clearance Center** to find daily deals and steals from top merchants on electronics, apparel, home décor, jewelry, sporting goods and much more.

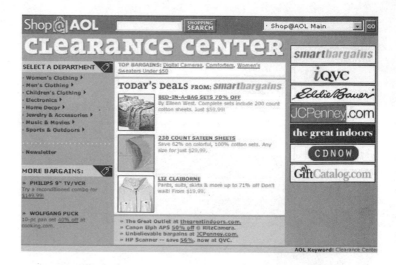

To find out more about special deals, great
savings and AOL member benefits visit AOL
Keyword: **Save Money.**

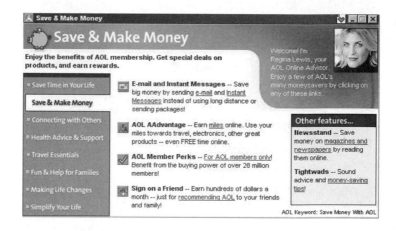

Gift reminder service

Fourteen days before your holiday or special occasion we'll e-mail you a reminder message. You also have the option for a second reminder, which can be sent to you four days before.

To register, just input the names and dates you need to remember via our simple add a reminder form located at AOL Keyword: **Reminder** under the "Create Your Reminder" button.

Wired Secret from Anna in AOL Member Services, Jacksonville, FL — Share your shopping wish list with friends and family!

When shopping on the Internet, sometimes I come across an item I'd like to receive as a gift! To quickly and easily share the item with friends and family, I click on the AOL favorite places heart and select the option to add the item to an e-mail. I can then send it off to as many people as I want — in hopes that they'll get the hint!

Online auctions

Do you like garage sales? Have something special you collect that you're always on the lookout for? Do you consider yourself a professional bargain hunter? If you answered yes to any of these, then online auctions are the place for you.

You may have heard of eBay, the online auction house. Go to AOL Keyword: **Auctions** or **eBay** to get there on AOL. Basically, it works like this: someone decides to sell an item and places a notice on the service. People who want it enter their bids.

You can check back to see if someone has outbid you and decide if you're willing to offer a higher price. At some point, after a set amount of time has passed or the seller is satisfied with the price, the auction is closed and the highest bidder wins. It's fun and a great way to get hold of hard-to-find items.

 What's your bid?

On any given day there are more than 5 million auctions at play each day in over 5,000 different categories on eBay. You simply won't believe the array of items up for grabs — from collectibles like an autographed Charlie's Angels doll to vintage jewelry, classic automobiles, old toys, sporting goods, hard to get concert tickets, musical instruments, furniture or even electronics like Palm Pilots or computers sold by companies with excess inventory.

There's certainly something for everybody! To learn the ropes of online auctions, a great place to start is AOL Keyword: **eBay Guide**.

Did you know?
Highest price ever paid
on eBay -

The highest priced item ever sold on eBay is a Gulf Stream II business jet, selling for $4.9 million. The General Dynamics Corp. jet sold for about three times eBay's previous record of $1.65 million paid for a Honus Wagner baseball card.

How to win at the online auction game

· When selling an item, the better your item description, the more you increase your chances that the item will fetch a higher price. The use of bold text has been shown to increase sales by as much as 35%. Also, don't forget to include a digital picture of the item.

· Experts say the best way to win at an auction is to look for auctions that are ending within hours, minutes or even seconds. That way, you can bid on an item and have less of a chance of someone outbidding you at the last moment.

Testimonial: Lisa Lillien poses with a few precious items she has purchased on eBay.

As a collector of old 70s TV items, advertising collectibles, stuffed lobsters and just general pop culture and kitsch, Lisa Lillien has made eBay one of her favorite sites on the Internet (AOL Keyword: **eBay**).

Clearly, eBay is a great place to consistently find items at reasonable prices! Over the past three years Lisa has purchased hundreds of items — everything from lunch boxes and old board games, to rare CDs, Wacky Packs and art. Having mastered the art of online auctions, Lisa has found many good bargains by using some clever techniques:

Incorporate common typos into a search — typing in "Partidge" rather than "Partridge," for example. You may find items that others do not, giving you the chance to get the items at a lower price.

Check the "going rate" for an item (for something you want to buy or sell) by searching "completed auctions" — here you will see what similar items sold for during the past three months.

Get the hottest ticket in town with AOL box office

AOL Box Office is the most comprehensive online event information and ticketing service, with all the scoop on local events like concerts, performing arts, sports, movies and family events in cities across the country. AOL Box Office takes you beyond the purchasing stage and provides localized and relevant promotions, exclusive special offers, entertainment news and updates, maps and directions and a whole lot more.

AOL Box Office users can find detailed information about the event of their choice by category, venue, or date and can purchase tickets through AOL Keyword: **Box Office** or on the Web at www.aolboxoffice.com. You can also find AOL Box Office in a number of areas throughout the AOL service — including the Sports, Entertainment, Parenting and Music channels, the AOL Local Guide and AOL Moviefone.

 ## Let's do it - time to travel

The AOL Travel channel is one of the most popular e-commerce destinations on the AOL service — and no wonder. From its main page, you can plan a trip and book flights, hotels, rental cars or cruises.

My brother planned his entire honeymoon online. He was so thrilled with the arrangements he lined up, for weeks he'd forward everyone in the family his travel itinerary in an e-mail titled "Check This Out!" He discovered lots of remote European hotels and restaurants and got some amazing deals.

Let's give it a try by searching for a flight. On the main screen, click on the **Plane** icon. Then click the box that says **Continue.** You'll be asked, "How flexible are your travel plans?" This helps pinpoint the best travel times and fares. Answer the question by clicking on one of the boxes.

You'll see a screen offering you boxes for your departure and destination cities or airports. If you are not sure what the name of the closest airport is, you can look it up by clicking on the link to your right.

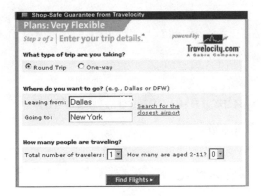

Fill in the city names (no states or countries needed). Select the number of travelers and the number of children traveling and click **Find Flights.**

The next screen will give you a selection of the lowest published fares. Select an airline and the following screen will allow you to select your departure date based on availability. Click on the date when you want to depart and then the date when you want to return.

You'll see an array of flight options at the best available prices.

Using the Internet to find your dream home

According to a recent survey by the National Association of Realtors, about 60% of all homebuyers are shopping for their houses on the Internet. There are currently an estimated 200,000 Web sites related to real estate. Traffic to these sites has surged in just the past few years, helping homeowners make educated decisions on what is likely to be the biggest purchase of their life.

The Internet can help you research every step of the homebuying process, from locating potential homes to finding out information on a neighborhood's school district, crime rate and the price of comparable homes.

The Web can also help you get approval for a loan and allow you to check your credit rating online. Many sites have links to lenders, credit reporting agencies, house inspectors and surveyors. Your best bet is to stick to larger sites like Homestore.com or Realtor.com, where they have everything under one roof. Visit the AOL House & Home channel or AOL Keyword: **Homestore.**

SECRETS DAY 5

· **Weddings:** My girlfriend planned and purchased almost everything for her wedding online. She's one of the most resourceful people I know and you can't imagine how much money she saved. If you're planning a wedding or know someone who is, visiting AOL Keyword: **Weddings** could be really worthwhile.

· **Newsletters:** You can search for deals and have them sent directly to you. In technology terms its called having something "pushed" to you. AOL has a Deals and Steals newsletter and many individual merchants — including airlines — do too. You can have them notify you on a regular basis. Visit AOL Keyword: **Newsletter Center** to subscribe. Little hint: When it comes to some sites, if you don't want to be notified of "special deals" make sure you do not opt in for this service (in some cases it may require unchecking a box).

· **Clip coupons online:** You know the coupon circulars in the newspaper? They're online too, and with one click you can print the ones you want. Go to AOL Keyword:

Coupons and you may find great savings at stores in your area every week.

· **Stop paying for out-of-town news:** A lot of people who've moved away from the place they grew up or lived for many years still subscribe to the hometown paper to keep up with what's going on. This is often expensive. With AOL, you can most likely read the paper online and save on out-of-town subscriptions and postage rates. Perform a search for the newspaper's name to find its Web site.

· **Special offers:** Sometimes when you sign on to the AOL service, the first thing you see will be a special offer for AOL members from one of America Online's e-commerce partners. These exclusive opportunities for everything from credit cards to computer software to digital cameras are often some of the best bargains available anywhere. Check them out and save.

· **Gift cards & monogramming:** Purchasing monogrammed gifts and attaching a gift card is a great thing to do online, because it helps guard against mistakes — what you type is what you or the person you're buying for, will get.

· **Product recalls:** Product recall information is also available online. Child product recalls — toys, car seats, cribs (the kinds of things you hear about on the news) are compiled on drspock.com which can be found at AOL Keyword: **Drspock**.

Hi-Wired
Quick checkout

▲America Online ●CompuServe ■Netscape

Does it take longer to type in your credit card and delivery information than it does to actually pick out the items you want? If so, you may be interested in Quick Checkout.

Enter your address, credit card information, and other basics, and we'll store the information so you can submit it to stores in a split second. You can change or update your profile whenever you need to and all the information will remain completely secure.

- **Step 1** Enter your zip code.
- **Step 2** Enter your credit card and shipping information.
- **Step 3** Create your shopping password.
- **Step 4** Begin one-click shopping!

At checkout time you will be able to add and choose different credit cards and shipping addresses. You can also update your credit cards anytime at: https://payment.aol.com or AOL Keyword: **Quick Checkout.**

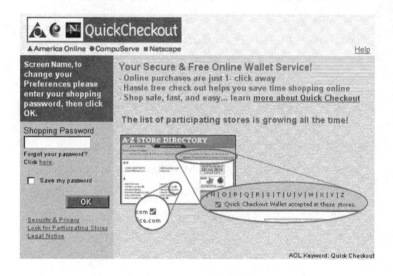

DAY 6

Get Going

If you're like me, between kids, work and general household activities, every day is a balancing act.

This is when the Internet can help simplify your life and make daily tasks such as managing your calendar or banking easier. The Internet can also help you in accomplishing longer-term goals like finding a job or pursuing continuing education.

Here are some of the ways the Internet can help you be more productive each day:

 ## My calendar

From PTA meetings to local concerts and family events, AOL's My Calendar is a great way to get organized and remember important events.

Go there by clicking the **My Calendar** icon on the Welcome Screen. You can also go to AOL Keyword: **Calendar**. My Calendar helps you track birthdays, holidays, the weather, horoscopes and family plans online.

To instantly add events to your calendar, click on any **add to my calendar** links on the AOL service or on the Web that interest you. You can also click on ad banners like the one shown below to add events to your calendar.

Finding a job and getting career advice

Whether you're looking to make a lateral move, looking to make a career switch or just looking... it makes sense to take advantage of all the resources the Internet has to offer.

With the dizzying number of job sites on the Internet, having a one-stop site to navigate takes some of the stress out of searching. Powered by Monster.com, AOL's Career & Work channel (AOL Keyword: **Careers**) brings it all together.

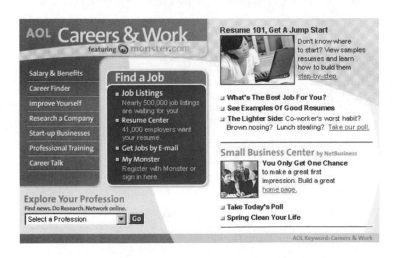

Search over 250,000 plus job postings by profession and location — even get job listings e-mailed to you. If you are trying to get the edge in a tight job market, you can get expert advice on building your resume step-by-step.

Tips for finding a job online

- How to know what job is right for you? Walk through the decision guide at AOL Keyword: **Career Finder**. The results may point you in a direction you never imagined.

- Want potential employers to see your resume? Go to AOL Keyword: **Resume** and post your resume on Monster.com.

- Curious about your market value? Check out AOL Keyword: **Salary and Benefits** to see what others in your field are making.

- Learning about companies you are interested in working for has never been easier — check out **Research a Company** at the Careers & Work channel.

- Chat with other job seekers in one of the hundreds of career-focused chats hosted on AOL each week at AOL Keyword: **Career Talk**.

Testimonial: "Want a new job? Get wired to get hired."

In these high-tech times, company recruiters are more frequently turning to the Internet to fill job openings. Sandra Corbett, a Virginia-based recruiting manager, talked with us about the effectiveness of the Internet in locating qualified candidates.

Q: What percentage of the new employees posts their resumes online?

A: Sandy: Approximately forty percent of our new hires in 2000 posted their resumes online.

Q: Do you post all your jobs online?

A: Sandy: Absolutely, it's probably the most cost effective way to reach a large audience. Not to mention the convenience factor for candidates — they can review job postings online, anytime and anywhere.

Q: How much of an effect has the Internet had on your recruiting?

A: Sandy: When I first started recruiting several years ago, the majority of the resumes posted online were for technical candidates. Now, with the popularity of the Internet, I can find qualified candidates (technical and non-technical) online and fill all of my vacancies.

Continuing education

Ok, so the kids are back at school. Now, maybe it's YOUR turn ... Learn a new language or the basics of bird watching. You name it, these days you can do it online. There are online resources to advance your career; to further your education and even earn a degree; and to pursue interests and hobbies of all kinds.

Some online courses are free, while others can cost $500 or more per credit hour earned toward a degree. You can't beat the convenience and studies show that distance learners do as well or better in courses and on tests than traditional students.

For more information on e-learning options and to gauge whether you have the self-motivated personality to pull it off, check out the new Online Campus area on America Online at AOL Keyword: **Online Campus.**

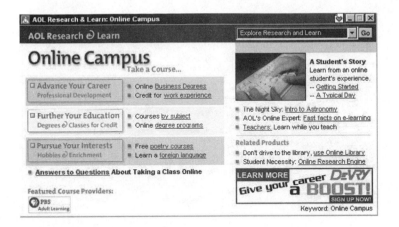

Government Guide

Did you know, online you could renew your driver's license or vehicle tags; check to see if the government owes you money; register for social security; send an e-mail to your Congressman or Senator; or check out local political issues?

Go to AOL Keyword: **Government**, the Internet's #1 consumer portal for government information to help make these tasks that much easier.

From birth to marriage to retirement, every major life event requires government record keeping. AOL's Government Guide can help you with these sometimes intimidating processes.

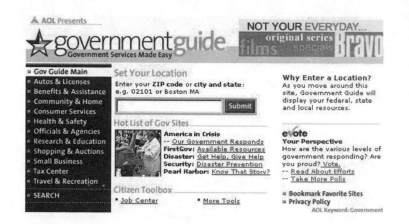

Keeping your financial house in order

To many people, the world of finance can seem like a jungle. Luckily, the AOL Personal Finance channel (AOL Keyword: **Personal Finance**) makes any financial environment more manageable.

AOL's Personal Finance channel gives you the tools to trade stocks, research companies and follow your own portfolio. It also provides tools to help you pay your bills, track your household budget and calculate your taxes.

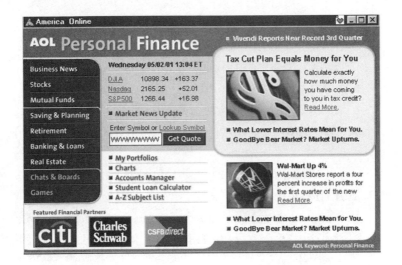

Personal finance tools for you

· Use AOL partner CitiBank to manage your finances online. CitiBank can help you plan major purchases, check your financial health, manage your mortgage and help with other aspects of your financial world.

· Students and parents can use CitiBank's Student Loan calculator and the College Budget Calculator to plan for college.

· AOL's QuickCash helps you e-mail
money to anyone with an e-mail address, so
it's great to send money to kids in college,
pay off purchases made on eBay, pay a debt
to a friend and send money overseas in a
secure and safe way.

· Calculate your taxes, download tax forms
and file online with AOL partner H&R Block.
You can also get tax law information and life
planning advice from H&R Block at AOL
Keyword: **Taxes.**

Why pay bills online?

· You never have to search for a stamp or
scramble to the post office to meet a
payment due date.

· You can pay bills anywhere, anytime,
which guards against late payments due
to travel and scheduling conflicts.

· Bill records are all kept in one place — no
more searching through files to find an
old check stub.

· Through e-mail confirmation, bill payers
have a solid record of when payments
were made and received.

NetBusiness

If you run your own small business — full-time or just as a way to make extra money — going online can help you get organized, stay on top of trends, access important information, take advantage of discounts on supplies, market your product or service, connect with other small business owners and even improve your bottom line.

Go to AOL Keyword: **Netbusiness** to get news, tips and tools for businesses as small as one to ten people. You can stay on top of important issues with stories from sources like Fortune Small Business, AOL Keyword: **FSB**. There is a wide range of advice from experts on subjects that run the gamut from advertising to finance to balancing work and family.

And you can promote your business online by easily creating your own Netbusiness Card, which lets potential customers know all about you and your company.

Plus, when you are ready, there are added resources that help you to manage your business and buy and sell products and services online.

E-mentoring

If you've always wanted to be a mentor, but feel like you don't have time to volunteer, e-mentoring may be the answer.

Programs like BestBuddies.org, a non-profit foundation started by the Shriver Family, allow you to have an e-mail relationship with someone who is mentally challenged. It's a wonderful way to make a difference from your home or office on your own time. Three little words: "You've Got Mail" can make someone's day and make a real impact over time. Visit AOL Keyword: **Mentoring** or go to www.mentoring.org.

Helping.org

AOL's Helping.org makes it easy for anyone on the Internet to give or volunteer. Formed in partnership with the nation's leading philanthropic organizations, Helping.org is a comprehensive philanthropy portal that allows you to search over 650,000 charities and more than 25,000 volunteer activities.

Even better, every organization on Helping.org has been researched and approved for inclusion on the site, so you know that the cause is worthwhile.

In the week following terrorist attacks on New York City and Washington D.C. on September 11, 2001, AOL members raised more than $20 million for relief efforts through Helping.org and other charitable giving through the service, demonstrating the generosity and sincere concern of AOL members around the world.

SECRETS DAY 6

· **Your forecast:** Want your AOL calendar to give you the weather forecast for the next week? When using My Calendar, find the Menu button on the top right by clicking on the **More** icon. Select **settings**, fill in the questions and *voila*—weather icons appear on your calendar. You can also use this feature when you travel.

· **Resume faux pas:** Worried about resume faux pas? Go to AOL Keyword: **Resume** and click on **Top Ten Resume Don'ts** for helpful hints on making your resume the best it can be.

· **Is your representative representing YOU?** Curious about how your representative votes on issues that matter to you? Go to AOL's Keyword: **My Government**, click on the **VoteNote** link and register for weekly updates on how your representative votes.

· **Want to renew your passport online?** No problem. AOL Keyword: **Passport** takes you the AOL Travel channel — click on the

Passport Services link on the right and presto, you are taken to the US State Department's official page that spells everything out.

· **Need a good laugh in the work place?** Go to AOL Keyword: **Workplace Humor** for Dilbertisms, career horoscopes and a co-worker compatibility test. And if you really can't take it anymore, try the humorous resignation letter generator.

· **Consider conducting a quarterly technology makeover.** Are your important/frequently used e-mail addresses up to date and stored in your online address book or on your buddy list? Is your printer ink running low and do you have an extra ink cartridge for the always inopportune time when the ink finally does run out? Are there new products or upgrades on the market you should be taking advantage of? Remember technology is supposed to SIMPLIFY not complicate your life. So be practical. Get what you're ready for — when you're ready for it. It took ten years for my parents to get rid of their rotary telephone. This year they got high-speed cable access. Now that's a makeover!

Hi-Wired
My portfolio

AOL's Personal Finance channel is the number one financial destination in cyberspace, providing millions of members with more than 245 million stock quotes per day.

Try the "My Portfolio" feature on the Personal Finance channel to make tracking your investments and retrieving stock quotes quick and easy. To set up your account, click on **My Portfolio** or go to AOL Keyword: **My Portfolio**.

Once you are on the My Portfolio page, click on **Create** and you will be prompted to name your portfolio.

Step 1 You can have fun with this - my friend named hers "Connie's Cash" for example. Click **Next**, then enter the information about your stocks in the boxes provided.

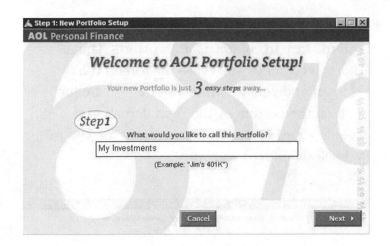

Step 2 When finished, click **Next** and you will be taken to a page where you can select additional indices or cash amounts to track.

Step 3 This helps you see how your investments fare in comparison to others. Once completed, click the **Finish** button on that screen and you are almost done — just click **OK** on the bottom of the next screen and voila, your portfolio page is ready for you to check whenever you want.

Special: "Wireless in a Week"

AOL Wireless
Your AOL On the Go

Surely you've seen them — people using wireless phones and two-way communications devices on trains and buses.

With so many activities keeping AOL members on the go — soccer practice, shopping, meeting friends and traveling for business — wireless phones, handheld computers and two-way communications devices are increasingly a "must" for parents, teenagers and professionals alike.

Of the more than 31 million America Online members, 72 percent own a wireless phone or pager. AOL members spend an average of 70 minutes per day connected to the AOL service on their PC, sending more than 228 million e-mails and 656 million instant messages every day.

With the increasing need for AOL members to be connected and stay connected, we're bringing you the convenience and peace of mind that come with being able to communicate real-time with friends and family. At the same time, you can access your favorite AOL features and services from a host of wireless products, in order to make your life easier and more productive. At AOL this is part of what we call the "AOL Anywhere" initiative.

In good times and bad times, it's comforting to know the people closest to you can be an e-mail or an IM away anytime, anywhere. In addition, AOL Anywhere products make it easy to access customized news, weather reports, sports scores, movie listings, driving directions, stock quotes and much more while you're on the go.

AOL Mobile Communicator™

The AOL Mobile Communicator™ is a two-way messaging device that looks like a pager with a miniature keyboard. It's portable, so AOL members can send and receive e-mails and instant messages anytime, from anywhere. And you can view your Buddy List® feature to see when fam-

ily, friends or colleagues are available online.

The AOL Mobile Communicator is also a great way for teens and parents to stay in touch throughout the day. Available on America Online at AOL Keyword: **Mobile Communicator**, the device makes it possible to send private messages anytime, anywhere without interrupting meetings, distracting others at restaurants or movies, or broadcasting to friends that you're talking to Mom.

Wireless phones

Now, your wireless phone can be used for more than just talking. With the AOL service on your wireless phone, you can access e-mail, instant messaging and the latest news headlines, as well as find a restaurant and check weather or local traffic reports. You can even check local movie times and buy tickets for the show.

Whether you're in a new city on a business trip, or hanging out with friends and making plans for a fun evening, all of these features are at your fingertips and easily accessible right from your phone.

AOL is working with a number of wireless carriers in the U.S. to bring these services to consumers across the country. Visit AOL Keyword: **Wireless** for more information on accessing AOL from your wireless phone.

And don't let the tiny keys on your wireless phone keep you from sending an e-mail or instant message. With AOL's T9® Text Input software, we make it easier for you to type words with your phone's numeric keypad. Traditional methods of typing on a wireless phone require you to press keys multiple times to get your desired letter. For example, to type the letter "L," you'd have to press the "5" key three times. Spelling the simple word "hello," would require you to make 13 key presses! T9 Text Input can cut in half the number of key presses necessary to spell words.

With T9 Text Input it takes just one key press per letter — in many cases — just like it would on a regular computer keyboard — to type words quickly and easily. Visit AOL Key-word: **T9 Text Input** to see a demo of how the T9 technology works. T9 Text Input is a stan-dard feature on more than 150 different wire-less phone models available worldwide — look for it on your phone.

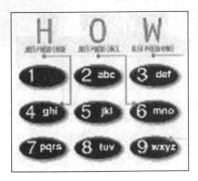

Personal digital assistants & handheld computers

A handheld computer or PDA (personal digital assistant) gives you the freedom to take your calendar, contact information and other important information with you when you're traveling or on the go, but what about your e-mail? Just as we've brought AOL ser-vices to wireless phone users, we give AOL members with PDAs easy access to their AOL e-mail as well as instant messaging and other popular features.

If your PDA uses the Palm, Pocket PC or Windows CE operating systems and you have a modem, you can download the AOL software (available at AOL Keyword: **Wireless**) to your PDA for FREE and you'll be on your way.

AOLbyPhone

With the convenience of the AOL by Phone service, you can check your e-mail, get the latest news, weather, restaurant reviews, movie listings and stock quotes plus do some last minute shopping from any telephone, simply by talking into your phone.

Using simple voice commands powered by the latest voice recognition technology, AOL-byPhone makes it possible for you to access your favorite AOL features anywhere you have access to a telephone. You talk, the technology does the rest.

Using AOLbyPhone is easy and really worth a try. You just dial a toll free number

(1-800-AOL-1234) where you are greeted by a
friendly voice that guides you to the information you want to find. For more information
on the AOLbyPhone service visit AOL Keyword: **AOLbyPhone.**

AOL Mail Alerts^{sm}

Our normal, daily activities don't always
allow us to keep an eye on our e-mail boxes,
but the AOL Mail Alerts^{sm} service helps
ensure that you'll never miss an important or
urgent e-mail again.

While away from your computer, the
AOL Mail Alerts service notifies you when
an e-mail has arrived in your AOL e-mail box
by sending a message to your text-enabled

digital wireless phone or alphanumeric pager. You can customize the AOL Mail Alerts service so that you're "pinged" each time you receive a new e-mail, or only when a specific e-mail arrives in your New Mail box (you can specify this by e-mail sender or subject). Visit AOL Keyword: **Mail Alerts** for more information on setting alerts.

AOL Keyword: Wireless

Ready to cut the cord? To find the device or service that best suits your needs, visit AOL Keyword: **Wireless** or go to **www.aol.com/aolwireless** to see the full array of wireless services and devices offered through AOL.

You'll find useful tips and tricks and other information on the latest wireless products and features. AOL Keyword: **Wireless** helps take the mystery and frustration out of buying a wireless phone.

By comparing the rate plans of all major wireless carriers, the AOL wireless store recommends the ideal carrier, phone and service plan to meet your needs and allows you to purchase the phone and service directly from the site. AOL Keyword: **Wireless** makes researching and buying wireless products and services more manageable than ever.

Notes

_____

_____

_____

_____

_____

_____

_____

_____

_____

_____

_____

_____

_____

_____

_____

_____

_____

_____

_____

DAY 7

Get a (Family) Life

 One of the best things about AOL is sharing it with others, especially children, as a way of spending time together and as a tool to help them learn.

How early can your child start to enjoy the online experience? I used to check my e-mail every morning with my infant daughter in my lap. To this day, when you ask her where her mom works, she doesn't say "America Online" — she says, "You've Got Mail!"

Indeed, there are more young people online than ever, and they're coming online at younger and younger ages. Twenty-five percent of recently polled AOL parents say their children are coming online as early as age two, with that number climbing to 90% by age six.

If you have young people in the house, you probably won't be surprised by the fact that AOL parents also report their children are more likely to "fight" over the computer than the telephone.

The online medium is really their medium and all indications are today's young people will grow up in an increasingly "connected" society.

A recent study of parents with children online indicated that most felt it had positive results:

- 71% said it had improved the quality of their children's homework;

- 70% said it had a positive effect on their children's skills for entering the job market someday;

- 64% said it had enhanced the quality of their children's overall written communication; and

- 56% said it had increased their children's interest in hobbies.

Many parents worry about letting their kids go online. In reality, the dangers of the online world are really no different than the offline world.

And the good news is, many of the same basic parenting instincts and rules apply and technology is on your side. The most important things parents can do to ensure a safe online experience for their children is to use parental controls technology and to spend time learning what your kids do online.

The AOL service offers Parental Controls. AOL Keyword: **Parental Controls**. These let you control the content your children can access, whether or not they're allowed to use e-mail and instant messaging and even how much time they spend online.

Having said that, there's no substitute for direct parental involvement. Ask your kids: "What are your favorite online places?" "Who are your online friends?" It's just like wanting to know where they are after school and who they're hanging out with.

Parental Controls put the power in the parents' hands where it belongs, ensuring your children are getting all the advantages of the online world while minimizing its hazards.

Let's do it - setting up Parental Controls

The first step is to set up a screen name for your child. Go to AOL Keyword: **Screen Name** and click where it says **Create Screen Names**. If you've already setup an AOL account for your child, you're in good shape. The following process will simply confirm the protocols put in place as part of the initial registration process covered in the first pages of this book. For everyone else, its worth taking a few minutes to make sure you've got up-to-date protection for your children.

A box will come up asking whether the screen name is for a child under 18. Click **Yes**, if appropriate, and a message will appear explaining some of AOL's online privacy and security policies for children. Take a few minutes to review them.

After you're done, click **Continue**, and onscreen directions will guide you through the same process of choosing a screen name that you went through for yourself. At the end of that process, you will be asked whether you wish to designate this as a "master screen name."

If the account is for your child, be sure to click **No**, so that he or she will not be able to alter the parental controls settings you pick. Once you've finished setting up the screen name, you're ready to setup parental controls.

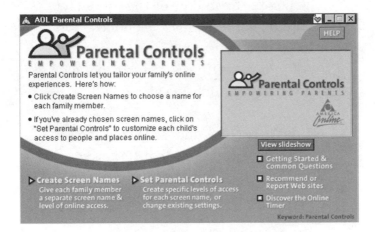

Sign on using the first screen name you've created (this is called the "master" screen name). Go to AOL Keyword: **Parental Controls**.

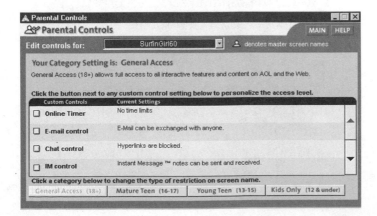

First, choose your child's screen name from the box at the top of the screen. Next, click on **Set Parental Controls**. This will connect you to a menu of choices.

The box in the middle of the screen lets you customize the settings you choose for your kids. Most people prefer to choose one of the standard settings at the bottom of the screen for their child's age group:

- **Kids Only** (12 & under) allows access only to age-appropriate interactive features, chat rooms, and content through AOL's Kids Only channel and the Web.

- **Young Teen** (13-15) allows access to age-appropriate interactive features and content on the AOL service and the Web. Access to premium services, private and member-created chat rooms, and instant message notes is blocked.

- **Mature Teen** (16-17) allows access to most interactive features and content on the AOL service and the Web. Web sites and newsgroups with explicitly mature content are blocked. Premium services are blocked.

You can choose any of these settings by simply clicking on the appropriate box. If you want to alter parts of these settings to customize them as you deem appropriate, click on the setting in question and read the options carefully. Select the one you want by clicking on the circle next to it. Then click **OK**.

Online Timer

One specific item you may want to set is AOL's exclusive Online Timer feature, which lets you specify what hours of the day children are allowed on the AOL service and how many hours a week you want them to spend online.

For example, parents can set the timer so their children can spend two hours online every evening, except Wednesday, which is set aside for piano practice. When you are done setting controls, you can click the menu screen closed and your changes will be saved.

To use the Online Timer:

Step 1   Go to AOL Keyword: **Parental Controls.**

Step 2   Click on **Set Parental Controls.**

Step 3 Select the screen name for which you are setting the Online Timer controls.

Step 4 Click on **Online Timer Control**.

Step 5 Follow the simple steps for the level of flexibility you prefer in setting time limits.

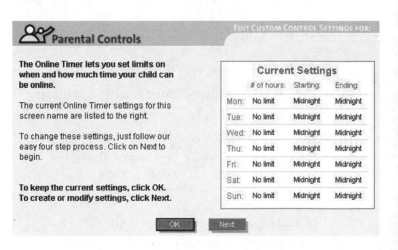

Exploring with your kids online

· **Kids ages 6 to 12**. There's an AOL just for kids. It's called Kids Only and it's free with your AOL subscription. From dinosaur clubs to the ability to create comic books, AOL Kids Only gives young people ages 6 to 12 the age-appropriate content they want and parents the peace of mind they need. AOL Keyword: **Kids.**

· **Teens**. It used to be that kids came home from school or for the summer and picked up the telephone. Now they race to the computer. Teens are some of the most active AOL users. But you need to be sure their activities are suitable for their age. Again, be involved. Spend time together at the computer. These days most teens are pretty tech-savvy, so odds are you'll learn a thing or two and they'll get a kick out of showing you. Teens — help out the adults! AOL Keyword: **Teens.**

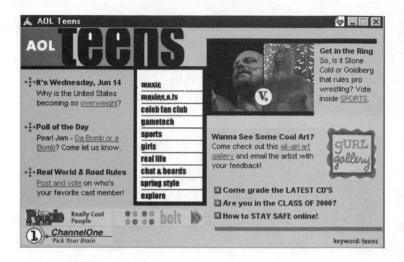

Off to college

While there are excellent learning resources for teens on the Web, one of the biggest things the Web offers are tools to help your children prepare for college.

They can take a virtual tour of almost any college or university that interests them and can even correspond with students to get a better feel for campus life.

There are also easy to use college decision guides on AOL to help your children pick the right college for them. Visit AOL Keyword: **College** to find out more.

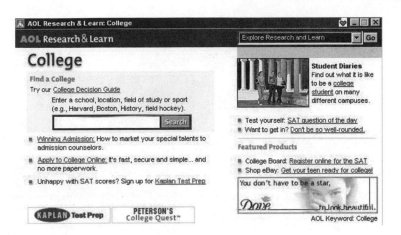

AOL Keyword: College

Homework help

One of the most useful features AOL offers is the free Ask-A-Teacher function, where volunteer real-life teachers are standing by to help. On AOL, we get over 13,000 questions a day!

Your kids can access this assistance through the Homework Help areas on either the Kids Only or Teens channels, or by going to AOL Keyword: **Ask-A-Teacher** and selecting their appropriate grade level from the menu.

For each grade level, there are several subject areas — math, history, etc. — along with message boards where children can post their questions and check back later for help finding the answers.

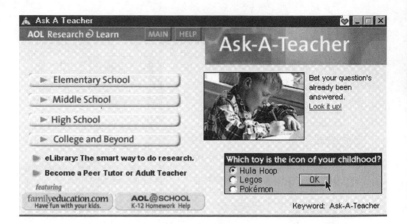

The high school Ask-A-Teacher section even features live help in special chat rooms setup by subject area.

Students just click on the **Live Teacher Help** button on the High School menu to get to these chats, which are open on weekday and weekend evenings. For additional resources on a wide range of educational opportunities for young people and adults, go to AOL Keyword: **Online Campus.**

And don't forget about the always-handy AOL Keywords: **Dictionary**, **Atlas** and **Thesaurus.**

AOL@SCHOOL   Surf the best educational resources

In this wired world, teachers, students, and parents are constantly looking for innovative ways to incorporate the Web into classrooms. But while over 95% of schools in the U.S. are now wired for the Internet, studies indicate that educators are not certain how best to make use of the Web's vast educational resources.

That's where **AOL@SCHOOL** comes in. Designed to help schools make the interactive medium a more effective part of the classroom experience, **AOL@SCHOOL** is a free online learning service that provides six, safe, age-appropriate learning portals with easy-to-follow connections to online content selected by educational experts.

These learning portals are specially designed to address the unique needs of different users including students in grades K-2, 3-5, middle school and high school, teachers and administrators.

If your child's school has not signed up, urge them to call us to get more information on the **AOL@SCHOOL** software, which is available free by calling 1-888-339-0767 or over the Web at http://www.school.aol.com.

AOL@SCHOOL

Testimonials: What educators are saying about AOL@SCHOOL

"Across the country, schools have struggled with the question of how to make the most of their Internet connections. By providing reliable, safe educational content in an easy to use format, AOL@SCHOOL provides tremendous help in answering that question." *Gerald Tirozzi, Executive Director of the National Association of Secondary School Principles.*

Special tips for grandparents

One of the best ways to keep in touch with your grandchildren is to go to one of the places they are most — online! Exchanging e-mails can be a terrific way to stay in close contact and ask the questions you want to know most: how's school, soccer, camp?

The online medium bridges distance and ages and is bringing families worldwide closer together.

Computers are giving older Americans a high-tech and easy way of doing their favorite activities, according to the 2001 AOL Senior Wired survey, some favorite activities include:

1. **Communication:** 95% of older Americans polled say they go online to e-mail and instant message.

2. **Research Information:** Older Americans find they are gaining independence by having access to a centralized source of information day or night, seven days a week, where they don't have to worry about business hours or finding transportation.

- 71% are frequently involved in information searches for themselves and their families.

- 49% research financial information and check their investments.

- 77% research travel and vacation options. This marks the biggest increase in what older Americans are doing online this year compared to one year ago.

- 58% look for medical and health information and resources.

3. **Shopping:** 60% shop online and buy products and services.

4. **Playing Games:** 44% play games (such as bingo, bridge and video games).

Testimonial: You're never too old. Pearl Kornbluth goes online for the first time at age 83! She didn't want a computer. Go online? No Way. But then her sons said, "You're 83. What are you waiting for?"

For most of the last decade, my sons tried to buy me a computer. I put them off. "Every year they come out with new features," I told them. "And every year the price goes down. I'll wait."

To celebrate the new millennium, my sons sent me a Dell computer. My first reaction was to treat it as an annoyance. But when your kids want to communicate with you, what mother can resist?

My sons' next gift: a computer tutor, the image of Tom Cruise. He came, he saw, he did not flee. He got me started — I am pleased to report it wasn't hard; AOL really is a snap. And then he did something that's become my signature.

He set my type font so big you'd swear you were reading an eye chart. Now my kids don't need to look at the top of the IM to know who's just dropped in. It's **MOM**, and she's got something they **MUST READ NOW**.

Researching your roots

Researching your family background is an adventurous and educational online activity to do with your grandchildren.

Online genealogy is one of the fastest growing activities online because it is empowering so many people to do things that used to take years and dozens of letters to government agencies, trips to local libraries and phone calls to long-lost friends and relatives.

There are more than a billion records posted online to help people piece together their past, including substitute Census Bureau information from 1890 which was lost in a 1921 fire and destroyed an entire generations family records.

Studies indicate more than 60% of Americans are interested in tracing their roots, and many of them are signing on for help.

To get started, gather as much information as you can about your family and visit AOL Keyword: **Genealogy**.

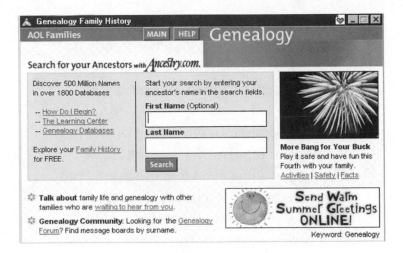

There, you'll be prompted to type in your family surname to begin tracing your roots.

Matching search results will be displayed from a number of databases including census records, birth, marriage and death records, military records, immigration and naturalization records and many more.

While some of the basic information is free, as you access more detailed records like the Census Bureau forms you will incur quarterly or annual subscription fees depending on what level of information you are seeking. The fees usually run about $40 per year. That compares to about $40 per hour for a professional genealogist.

The success stories are amazing. One woman we know discovered her family had a genetic blood disorder that was being passed down from generation to generation.

She did some research online to identify her extended family; they all went to be screened and some even had life saving preventative surgery. Whatever the impetus for tracing your family history — a child's school paper, a death in the family — it seems the way we research our past will never be quite the same.

 ## Keeping your online neighborhood safe

Like anyplace else, the online world has a few dark corners. AOL works very hard to protect our members from online scams and other potential hazards, but we urge you to do your part as well.

A lot of this comes down to common sense — knowing who you're dealing with — and using the features that AOL has built to allow you to control your online experience. To this end, here's some good advice.

✉ E-mail safety tips

- **Use mail controls to block junk e-mail:** As the Internet world grows, so do the problems of junk e-mail--unsolicited, unwelcome e-mail. In addition to our ongoing efforts to block this unwelcome e-mail, there are some simple things that you can do too.

- **Official AOL mail:** Determine if an e-mail is Official AOL Mail by looking for a blue envelope in your mailbox, a blue border around the mail and the "Official AOL Mail" seal. Go to AOL Keyword: **Official AOL Mail** to learn more.

- **Set mail controls:** With the Mail Controls feature, you can control the e-mail you and your children receive. You can block specific screen names or Internet addresses from sending you mail. You can also block the exchange of mail with attached files or pictures. For more information, go to AOL Keyword: **Mail Controls.**

· **Don't open hyperlinks or attachments from strangers:** Online scam artists will often send people hyperlinks or attachments they claim are official AOL instructions, special offers or the like. Don't believe them. If you get e-mail from someone you don't know with a hyperlink in it, don't click on it. If it has an attachment you're not expecting, don't download it. These are sometimes tricks used to spread computer viruses that could harm your computer or invade your personal privacy.

 ## Additional safety tips

· Don't give your AOL password to just anyone. It's fine to give out your screen name (e-mail address). Kids should not give out their screen names without their parents' permission.

· Create an alternate screen name for chat rooms and for posting online personals. Go to AOL Keyword: **Screen Names,** and click **Create a Screen Name.** Refer to Day 1 for more on this.

· Select a password that combines letters and numbers. AOL Keyword: **Password** has more information on creating secure passwords.

· For added security, use different passwords for each screen name on your account.

· Report all offending e-mail to screen name TOSemaill or by using AOL Keyword: **Notify AOL.**

 ## Safety tips-for kids

· Don't give your AOL password to anyone, even your best friend, brother, or sister.

· NEVER tell anyone your home address, telephone number, or school name without getting your parent's permission first. Don't type this information into a Web page online either, without checking with your parents.

· If someone says something that makes you feel unsafe or funny, don't respond to them. Tell your parents or a teacher and AOL. Find out how at AOL Keyword: **Kids Help.**

·NEVER say you'll meet someone in
person without first asking for your
parents' permission.

·Don't accept information from strangers
(e-mail, files, Web page addresses or
hyperlinks).

AOL Keyword: **Neighborhood Watch** has more
information on all of these important topics.

SECRETS DAY 7

Keep your kids learning at home

Have your child write e-mail letters about
their summer vacation to relatives, friends or
teachers. This will keep their spelling, gram-
mar and general writing skills fresh.

AARP
on AOL

Older Americans can get a fast, free benefits checkup

Created by The National Council on the
Aging, Benefits CheckUp is a free, easy-to-use
service that identifies federal and state assistance programs for older Americans.

Researching these programs used to be a
time-consuming, frustrating experience. The
National Council on the Aging created Bene-
fitsCheckUp to help older adults quickly
identify programs that may improve the
quality of their lives.

Family and friends can also obtain facts
about benefits their loved ones may qualify
for. You may be surprised to learn what benefits are available to you, regardless of your
income. Visit AOL Keyword: **Benefits Checkup.**

Wired secret from April in AOL Member Services, Jacksonville, Fl.

Save 10% off your monthly AOL bill. A great money saver for senior citizens is only a few clicks away on AOL. AARP members receive a 10% discount off the AOL standard pricing plan. Just visit AOL Keyword: **AARP** to fill out a simple request and you will be notified via e-mail when the discount has been approved and applied.

Are you deleting your own history?

Verbal history has always played a significant part in how we pass down information from generation to generation. These days, so much of our correspondence is by e-mail instead of hand written letters.

The good news is with millions of e-mails exchanged daily, many of us have an even greater play-by-play account of our daily lives. A digital diary or sorts, sometimes called a Web log or "blog." That's if we're not inadvertently deleting it.

After all, when our grandchildren go to the attic, they probably won't find a box of old letters and they certainly won't be able to read deleted e-mails.

So, here's a low-tech solution: Consider saving select e-mails on a disk or at a minimum, print some of your e-mail correspondence and keep them in a box in the attic.

Hi-Wired
Planning for retirement

Not only are computers and the Internet providing users with high-tech ways of doing their favorite activities — they are also helping to take the guesswork out of the once arduous take of financial planning.

Anybody saving for retirement inevitably asks themselves a few fundamental questions... "Am I saving enough? How much do I need to retire? Is it too early or too late to start saving?" AOL's Personal Finance channel has some handy retirement calculators to answer these questions and many, many more, including: "What will my expenses be? How much will my savings will be worth? How will inflation impact my savings? What if tax laws change? What about Social Security? How much do I need to save to become a millionaire?"

A good retirement calculator starts by asking the question, "How much will my savings be worth?" This is a good way to see what your savings will amount to over the long haul.

As illustrated below, you'll be asked to enter some basic information related to your current investments and state and federal tax rates. Once you have entered in all relevant information, click on the **results** button and your customized financial projections will appear in a matter of seconds. You can even view the results in a graph.

How much will my savings be worth?

| ☑ inputs | ! results | ▦ graphs | ? explanation |

View Single-Page Format

Amount You Have Invested	$ 5000
Rate You Can Earn	6.0 %
Additional Deposits	$ 300
⦿ Monthly ○ Quarterly ○ Yearly	
Years Invested	30
Your Federal Tax Rate	30 %
Your State Tax Rate	8 %
Inflation Rate	3 %

results ⇨

Visit AOL's Personal Finance channel or AOL Keyword: **Retirement** to find a number of other financial calculators to help you plan for your golden years.

Congratulations: you're wired!

I hope this book is only the beginning of your online journey. There's plenty more to learn about the constantly expanding world of the Internet. We're always updating the AOL service based on your feedback. The best way to stay on top of what's new is to keep exploring. You'll find even more features and areas designed to keep you connected with the people you care about most and make your everyday life easier and more convenient.

On behalf of everyone at America Online, thanks for taking the time to use this book, and here's looking forward to connecting with you again soon.

Enjoy!
Regina Lewis

Feedback: We want to stay in touch and hear what you find helpful about this book, and what you'd like to know more about. Visit AOL Keyword: **Wired in a Week** for ongoing updates, additional tips and to view recent TV appearances.

Emergency Technology Tip Sheet

One of the most important parts of responding to emergencies is being prepared. E-mail and the Internet can be a critical resource. Take these simple steps today to make sure you are "Internet ready" in case of an emergency:

1. Create a list of important e-mail addresses: Just as you keep a list of important phone numbers in case of emergencies, you should develop a list of e-mail addresses including friends, family and other emergency contacts. Save them online as a Buddy List Group and make multiple copies and keep them at home, at work and in a purse or wallet that you carry with you. AOL Keyword: **Address Book.**

2. Design a family Web site: If someone needs to track down your family or friends in a crisis, a family Web site listing important phone numbers and e-mail addresses can be a critical resource. The site can also include instructions on how to respond during a crisis, including maps, etc. Let your neighbors, co-workers and others know the address. AOL Keyword: **Hometown.**

3. Get a group: You can also create an AOL Group for your loved ones which can link to your family website and provide a private or public forum where you can all "gather" before, during and after any major events. Part of your emergency plan might include checking in with the "group" as soon as you can. AOL Keyword: **Groups**.

4. Consider getting a second phone line or broadband access: To ensure Internet access during an emergency, consider getting a second phone line so you can be online and use the phone at the same time. High-Speed Broadband Access runs on cable lines, DSL and satellite, providing another reliable means of communication which may work even if/when local phone lines are down. AOL Keyword: **High Speed**.

5. Make sure you have a charged cell phone or wireless device: Wireless phones and devices (PDA's, two-way pagers, etc.) also run on separate networks and provide alternative means of communication. It's important to make sure these are charged at all times. Keep or donate old cell phones -- as long as it's charged, dialing 911 still works even if you don't have a current service contract. AOL Keyword: **Wireless.**

6. Think local: America Online will elevate relevant online resources in a crisis, so you'll have quick access. In addition, it makes sense to familiarize yourself with local online resources, so you know where to go for customized news and information on nearby emergency resources such as hospitals, community centers and evacuation routes. AOL Keyword: **Local.**

7. Learn how to identify hoaxes: E-mail hoaxes and "urban legends" can increase during a crisis. Keep in mind reputable charities don't solicit donations via e-mail. If you receive an e-mail asking for a charitable donation, be suspect. Your best bet is to go directly to the charitable sites or link to them from America Online. AOL Keyword: **Helping.org.** Also, if you're curious about the validity of a story e-mailed to you, check out AOL Keyword: **Urban Legends.**

Notes

My online life

Life is filled with passwords. You probably can't remember them all. We thought writing them down on a single page might be helpful.

FAVORITE SITES

This is for sites on the AOL service and the Web that you like to visit. You'll want to write down the keyword or web address.

Site	How to Get There

KEYWORDS

You went there. You liked it. Make it easy to go back.

Site	How to Get There

FRIENDS & FAMILY

Screen names of family, friends and co-workers.

Index

●●●●●●